STENDHAL

by
MARCEL GUTWIRTH

Stendhal's peculiar place in the pantheon of great novelists reflects the unusual concord of warring elements in the writer's own breast: naive and blasé, tremulously brash, tenderly incisive. The novels of his maturity arise from a sense of the primacy of politics, transcended in romance; they celebrate the heroic, and persuasively chronicle its prompt demise; they exalt lucidity and blast the fools in power, but lucidity teaches them none but fools can long survive in the race *for* power. A man of many masks who could swathe passion in irony and sincerity in airiness, Stendhal, who entrusted his fame to the wheel of fortune, has earned a secure footing in a world that has not yet quite broken with either reason or passion.

TWAYNE'S WORLD AUTHORS SERIES
A Survey of the World's Literature

Sylvia E. Bowman, Indiana University

GENERAL EDITOR

FRANCE

Maxwell A. Smith, Guerry Professor of French, Emeritus
The University of Chattanooga
Former Visiting Professor in Modern Languages
The Florida State University

EDITOR

Stendhal

(TWAS 174)

TWAYNE'S WORLD AUTHORS SERIES (TWAS)

The purpose of TWAS is to survey the major writers—novelists, dramatists, historians, poets, philosophers, and critics—of the nations of the world. Among the national literatures covered are those of Australia, Canada, China, Eastern Europe, France, Germany, Greece, India, Italy, Japan, Latin America, New Zealand, Poland, Russia, Scandinavia, Spain, and the African nations, as well as Hebrew, Yiddish, and Latin Classical literatures. This survey is complemented by Twayne's United States Authors Series and English Authors Series.

The intent of each volume in these series is to present a critical-analytical study of the works of the writer; to include biographical and historical material that may be necessary for understanding, appreciation, and critical appraisal of the writer; and to present all material in clear, concise English—but not to vitiate the scholarly content of the work by doing so.

Stendhal

By MARCEL GUTWIRTH

Haverford College

Twayne Publishers, Inc.   ::   New York

Library of Congress Catalog Card Number: 77-120508

ABOUT THE AUTHOR

Marcel Gutwirth was born in Antwerp, Belgium, of American parents in 1923, and received his elementary and high school education in that country. After serving overseas with the U.S. Army in World War II, he took his A.B., M.A., and Ph.D. degrees at Columbia University. He has taught French and General Humanities at Haverford College since 1948. A Fulbright post-doctoral scholar in Paris in 1953-54, and a Fellow of the American Council for Learned Societies in Paris in 1964-65, he contributed articles ranging from Montaigne to Sartre to French and American journals, and is the author of *Molière ou l'invention comique* (Paris: Minard, 1966) and *Jean Racine: un itinéraire poétique* (Presses de l'Université de Montréal, 1970). He is married to Madelyn Katz; she is now Professor of French at West Chester State College (Pa.). They have three children: Eve, Sarah, Nathanael.

For Madelyn

Acknowledgments

The three major novels—*Le Rouge et le Noir, Lucien Leuwen, La Chartreuse de Parme*—are quoted from consistently in the following English language editions, respectively:

M. R. B. Shaw's translation in Penguin Classics (referred to as Penguin).*

Louise Varèse's two-volume translation in New Directions (referred to as *The Green Huntsman,* for tome I; and *The Telegraph,* tome II). Reprinted by permission of New Directions Publishing Corporation.

C. K. Scott Moncrieff's translation in the Anchor Book Series (referred to as Anchor). Permission of Liveright Publishers, New York. Copyright renewed 1953 by George Scott Moncrieff.

Lamiel is quoted from in T. W. Earp's translation (Direction 23).

Otherwise the translations are mine, mainly from the two-volume Pléiade edition of the tales and the novels (which include the unfinished novel *Le Rose et le Vert, Armance,* and the novella "Mina de Vanghel"), referred to as *Romans* (title of the work quoted); from the Pléiade volume *Œuvres intimes* (referred to as *OI),* which groups together *The Life of Henry Brulard,* the *Journal,* the *Memoirs of Egotism,* and the *Privilèges* (among the works quoted from).

---

* Regrettably titled: *Scarlet and Black,* a bit of pedantry steadily ignored in my references, which stick to the established cadences of *The Red and the Black.*

Preface

Little can be written today concerning a writer of the stature of Stendhal that could do more than sum up what is already known. All that a new work can do is to arrange the facts and the author's own reflections upon them in an order that may lead the reader to a fresh realization of the good fortune that is already his—to count that great man as one of his acquaintance. To the reader fortunate enough to be able to look forward to a *first* reading of *The Red and the Black* or *The Charterhouse of Parma* these pages will do no more than give a feeble indication of the pleasures in store.

Stendhal wrote a great deal, all of it of interest and much of it of great profit, but in a study devoted to his place in the select company of World Authors I felt that the novels were foremost, together with the autobiographical writings that throw them in such vivid relief by the light they shed on their complex bonds to the writer. The *Life of Rossini,* that of Napoleon, the writings on music, on the fine arts, on travel, the political reflections in the English periodicals, *The Italian Chronicles,* I have left to the converted reader's further curiosity. The pages that follow are centered almost exclusively on the works that gave Stendhal's name resonance for the common reader (in the richest sense of that appellation).

The Prologue of this study is devoted to the uses Stendhal made of his own life in his autobiographical writings. The persona or *mask* he invented in the restless search for the *person* he could never quite compass, invites and even demands comparison with the heroic self-recreations upon which he embroidered his tales, and the "play of masks" gives us some clue to the characteristic *démarche* of his imagination.

The Epilogue echoes this concern with the protean metamorphoses of the self, pursued this time beyond Henri Beyle's own life, amid the capricious games of posthumous fortune. A writer is as much a creature of the reader's own imagination as he is the shaper and the guide of that imagination. When we say "Stendhal" today, thought must be taken of what from Taine to Georges Blin we owe to the recreative exegesis.

Sandwiched in between, five chapters seek to probe the major novels (primarily) from a variety of angles. "The Pistol Shot" is dedicated to the political underpinnings of the three great works—*The Red and the Black, Lucien Leuwen, The Charterhouse of Parma.* "Terra Incognita" examines the Stendhalian hero with respect to his destiny of love. "The Bog" is the survey of the false Powers, Thrones, and Dominations through whose ranks the hero must tread a perilous way. "Euclid" bestows a nod on the hero's few scattered allies, to establish their essential kinship with the faith of the Enlightenment in certain knowledge expressed with clarity, honesty, and precision. "Brief Candle," finally, reviews the meteoric course of the hero's adventure, set by the demands of greatness in an age of mediocrity, fated like the life of Achilles to atone for transcendent brilliance with untimely demise.

The reader will find in this book as much of Stendhal as I was able to bring into it, quoting the text upon every occasion that gave excuse for letting him speak in his own voice (albeit in translation). This seemed the best way to open or renew the acquaintance which I take to be the sole aim of this enterprise.

My thanks go, in closing, to Sylvia Bowman for her patience with a manuscript too long in the making; to Grace Stoddard for deciphering my hand with unfailing good humor; to Haverford College for defraying the costs, through its Committee on Faculty Research and Study, of the preparation of this text; to the College librarians for the cheerful alacrity with which they let their time and resources be plundered in the service of scholarship.

M. G.

Contents

Chronology

1783   January 23, birth of Henri Beyle in Grenoble.

1799   September 15, earns the first prize in mathematics, in his third year at the *Ecole centrale,* and leaves for Paris in October.

1800   End of January, goes to work for his cousin Pierre Daru at the Ministry of War. In May leaves for Italy, which he reaches by June. Named aide de camp to General Michaud in 1801, takes leave by year's end, and resigns from the service in 1802.

1805   May 8, leaves Paris with the actress Mélanie Guilbert for Marseilles, where they live together for a year while he works in the export business (in groceries).

1806- Resides in Brunswick as aide to the War Commissioner and
1808   administrator of the Imperial estates in Germany.

1809   Sojourn in Vienna and mission to Hungary in the service of Count Daru.

1810   The peak of his Napoleonic career: auditor to the Council of State and Inspector of Crown Buildings.

1811   Second stay in Milan; affair with Angelina Pietragrua.

1812- Mission to Moscow, marked by distinguished service in the retreat
1813   from that city.

1814   Assists Count de Saint-Vallier in a bootless defense of Grenoble against the allied invasion.

1814- Third and last stay in Milan, where he lives on his military
1821   retirement pension. *The Lives of Haydn, Mozart, and Metastasio* (Paris, 1814)

1817   *History of Painting in Italy; Rome, Naples, and Florence.*

1818   March 4, first phase of the long unhappy love affair with Mathilde Viscontini Dembowski, his Métilde, which leads to no physical intimacy, and ends with his dismissal, heartbroken, in 1821.

1819   June 20, death of his father, Chérubin Beyle. Learns that he has been left practically penniless.

1821   June 13, leaves Milan under suspicion by the Austrian police of *carbonaro* activities.

1822   *De l'Amour (On Love)*

1823   *Racine and Shakespeare; Life of Rossini.*

1824 Liaison with Countess Curial. Seventeen articles on the Paris *Salon* in the *Journal de Paris.*

1825 *Racine and Shakespeare II.* Growth of his reputation as a brilliant conversationalist.

1826 End of the liaison with Clementine Curial (Menti). First stay in London. Begins work on *Armance.*

1827 *Armance.* July 20, departure for Italy (Genoa, Naples, Florence, Rome). He is expelled from Milan by the Austrian police (January, 1828).

1829 Brief and passionate love affair with Alberthe de Rubempré (Delacroix's cousin). *Roman Journal (Promenades dans Rome).* October, begins work on *The Red and the Black.* "Vanina Vanini" in *Revue de Paris.*

1830 January 27, Giulia Rinieri declares her love, she later gives herself to him, but he requests in vain her hand in marriage from her tutor Commendatore Berlinghieri. September 25, Named consul in Trieste by Louis-Philippe (King of the French since July). November 13, *The Red and the Black.*

1831 Rejected by the Austrian government as consul to Trieste; he is named to the lesser post at Civita-Vecchia, in the Papal States.

1832 Writes (but does not publish) *Memoirs of an Egotist (Souvenirs d'Egotisme).*

1834- Writes (but does not finish) *Lucien Leuwen.*
1835

1835- Writes (but does not finish) *The Life of Henry Brulard.*
1836

1837 Writes (but does not finish) *Le Rose et le Vert.* Works on a life of Napoleon, and publishes a few more of the Italian tales, published posthumously under the collective title *Chroniques italiennes.*

1838 *Memoirs of a Tourist.* Writes *The Charterhouse of Parma* in two months.

1839 *The Charterhouse of Parma* appears in April. He leaves Paris and returns to Civita-Vecchia, where he works on *Lamiel.*

1840 A last romance: the mysterious Roman flame "Earline." October 15, reads Balzac's "rave" on *The Charterhouse of Parma* in *La Revue Parisienne,* and starts work on the suggested revisions.

1841 March 15, first apoplectic fit. "I have tussled with the void." November 8, beginning of his last stay in Paris.

1842 Works on the Italian tales ("Suora Scolastıca.") March 22, felled by apoplexy in the street. Dies the next day in his hotel room without regaining consciousness. Buried the following day in Montmartre Cemetery.

PROLOGUE
A Play of Masks

A S he looked into his mirror the French consul in the backwater Papal town of Civita-Vecchia would see reflected the somewhat coarse features of a heavy-set man in his fifties, disappointed but mercifully unembittered at the undistinguished end of a career of public service that had at one time shown great promise. Perhaps he did not see behind the mask of that kindly, harassed, and too often desultory official the face of a writer destined to equal and some day overtake the fame of Balzac, in whose gigantic shadow he was quite content to remain lost to the eyes of his contemporaries. Surely not—for he looked on his writings as tickets in a lottery, whose winning number would be just this: *to be read still in 1935.* But certainly he knew, as his autobiographical writings amply testify, how far removed the spiritual reality lay behind that benign, deceptive appearance. The dreamer Dominique, Mocenigo the cool and calculating observer, the nonconformist Henry Brulard, Banti the perplexed lover, and above all the writer Stendhal all strain against the paunchy, slightly doleful exterior of the impecunious aging bachelor Consul Beyle, who was to die one day of apoplexy on a Paris street.

Stendhal reinvented his life several times, both in fictional and nonfictional accounts. Yet a writer feeds as much perhaps on the arbitrary circumstances of his existence, on his *situation* (which is also his *fatum),* as he does on their felt and reimagined reality—on his reappropriation of them, that is, as chosen destiny. Before we look into the *Life of Henry Brulard* and the *Memoirs of an Egotist* a glance might be in order, therefore, at the facts of Beyle's life, such as they might be given us by an uninventive, uninterpretive Dictionary of National Biography—as the public account of a public life. For it is not a negligible element of Stendhal's contribution to European letters that this most idiosyncratic of temperaments, this most uncompromising of detached observers, this fervent escapist and ardent libertarian earned what living he did earn as a well-traveled official of the French State under Napoleon and Louis-Philippe. Thus the eye he cast on the scene of his fictional worlds was an eye trained to see through official prose, and to sort out what, in a given situation under his jurisdiction, could and had to be *acted* upon. It is as one who had been called upon to act, though he preferred to dream, that he plunged the modern novel into contemporary reality; not, as did Balzac, to lose himself in it with horrified fascination, but to hold it disdainfully and amusedly to account for falling so far short of the lowliest of dreams.

I *Daguerreotype of the Artist*

Henri Beyle was born in Grenoble in the year 1783, of Chérubin Beyle, a lawyer of middling circumstances, and Elisabeth Gagnon—fifteen years her husband's junior—the daughter of a prominent, cultivated, well-to-do town physician. His mother died in his seventh year; the father weathered the blow stoically, but turned to a gloomy devotion, in keeping with the character of the old maid sister-in-law, Séraphie Gagnon, to whom he turned for help in running the household and raising his children. Resentment at the naysaying that had replaced the open and cheerful and loving ways he remembered as his mother's set the youngster at odds with his now clerical-dominated home, and his rebelliousness, by a quirk of history, was further incited by the Revolution that had broken out in Paris the previous year. The political struggle against the regime of a monarchy buttressed by ecclesiastical authority echoed in the breast of the little boy who felt himself oppressed by the tyranny of aunt Séraphie, reinforced by the presence of a much-resented tutor, the Abbé Raillane. Lifelong republican and anticlerical convictions appear to have grown from those childhood seeds. School gave him an escape from a home life that had grown both oversheltered and repressive, and distinction in mathematics, for the study of which the boy developed a fervent enthusiasm, provided the longed-for key to his freedom: removal to Paris in 1799, at the age of sixteen, to compete for admission to the Ecole polytechnique—then as now the finest school of mathematics in France. Mathematics had served its purpose, however: once removed from his hated Grenoble, grubby embodiment of provincial conformity, the youth failed to make an appearance at the school and gave himself up in earnest to dreams of literary glory, aspiring as he did to fill all at once the succession of both Molière and Don Juan.

But Grenoble did not lose its lifelong hold on its errant and ungrateful son: his cousin Pierre Daru, the powerful head of a clan whose fortunes were to rise impressively with the Empire, of which the future Count and Minister of State was a hardworking, able, and efficient mainstay, soon rescued him from obscurity and neglect. The puny young fellow, who allied grandiose aspirations with the wobbliest attainments (like the hero of *The Red and the Black,* Julien Sorel, he was to spell *cela* with two *l*'s on his first day at his desk in the War Ministry), was taken in hand firmly and patiently by his eminent kinsman, to whom he owed both perquisites of a moderately successful Parisian existence: access to a salon, and a modest claim on the State budget.

Daru was kinder to his young cousin than he knew: in 1800, in his capacity as head commissioner of military ordnance he sent Beyle to Italy, which he reached, on horseback, across the Saint-Bernard Pass. It was love at first sight. The thrill of danger, the stamp of heroism allied with melting tenderness, the music of Mozart and Cimarosa, a landscape of voluptuous repose, animated by the presence of brilliant and beautiful women, quite took the seventeen-year-old second lieutenant's breath away. The lovemaking, in his case, was to remain vicarious this time; but Milan from that day formed the lodestar of his existence, charged for him with all that could make life worth living—as recorded in his chosen epitaph (and ultimate impersonation): *Arrigo Beyle, MILANESE!*

A brief tour of duty as cavalry lieutenant and general's aide de camp completed Beyle's novitiate, in the fashion that was to form the pattern of his career. Disenchantment with the coarseness of army life soon overcame the excitement of a brilliant uniform; Lieutenant Beyle first returned to Grenoble on sick leave and was then back in Paris in 1802, having quite unceremoniously resigned from the army to devote himself to his literary studies. There followed an interlude of four years of intensive reading in literature and philosophy, of fervid theater-going with the object of mastering the craft of playwriting, and of vast and unavailing efforts at putting together a number of plays in verse, destined, alas, never to leave the drawer. A dash to Marseilles in 1805 to learn the ways of the export business and enjoy the fruits of his first love conquest, the actress Mélanie Guilbert, convinced him after a year that he was not cut out for the placid waters of commerce and undisturbed domesticity. Pierre Daru reappeared on his horizon, now the head of all French military ordnance. Properly placated, he resumed his patronage of his troublesome young cousin, who in 1806 was appointed Commissioner of Supplies in Brunswick, and in 1808 administrator of the imperial domains in that region of occupied Germany. In 1809 he accompanied Pierre Daru to Vienna as War Commissioner; 1810 brought the apex of his administrative career: State Auditor in the War Bureau and later Inspector of the Crown Buildings.

Throughout this period he paid largely silent and hopeless court to Countess Daru, the wife of his protector, whose feelings for him he feverishly scrutinized in his journals, noting every slightest hint of apparent ebb and flow. In 1811 a few months' leave in Italy assured him the conquest of Angela Pietragrua, the impetuous beauty whose love life,

[3]

in his earlier stay in Milan ten years before, he had had to be content to admire from afar. Her genius for intrigue—trysts cloaked in secrecy, hurried removal of her lover to Bologna to elude the suspicions of a supposedly jealous husband—quite fulfilled the requirements of energy in the service of passion which, in Beyle's eyes, made Italy the land of love.

But the end of the Napoleonic adventure was approaching. In 1812 Beyle traveled to Moscow with the invading Grand Army as Commissioner of War Supplies, and was given the chance to display his nerve and resourcefulness in organizing his share of the retreat. His overwhelming feeling was one of revulsion at the grossness and empty boastfulness of his fellow officers, a collection of hulking and mean-spirited swashbucklers *(sabreurs)*. In 1813 he served in Silesia. By the year's end he was recalled from sick leave in Milan to help reorganize the defense of the Dauphiné province against the Allied invasion. 1814 saw him back in Paris, balked out of his post by local inertia in a hopeless military situation. The Restoration of the Bourbons sent him off to Milan, to live on a small annuity inherited from the Gagnon side, eked out by his retirement half-pay. Now at last he gave himself over entirely to the life of voluptuous dilettantism which formed his stated ideal: *la chasse au bonheur.*

The idleness was more apparent than real, however. This was the time of his third and decisive apprenticeship. Paris and Milan at the turn of the century had taught him the nature of his dream and faced him with the realities of salon life and career that were indispensable steps toward its attainment. A decade of increasing practical responsibilities had followed, backed up by the steady enlargement of his literary and intellectual baggage. It culminated in the long-delayed conquest of Angela Pietragrua: the dreamer, the writer, the man of action had still not merged into an altogether victorious amalgam—but the distance between dream and action had been partly bridged, the greater self-confidence of the Napoleonic administrator was giving the future novelist some experience worth reflecting upon (albeit no more than that of his incurable gullibility). Milan, between 1814 and 1821, was to complete his education. As a writer, it brought him his first whiff of printer's ink. With the *Lives of Haydn, Mozart & Metastasio* (1815), the two volumes of the *History of Painting in Italy* and *Rome, Naples, and Florence* (both published in 1817) Beyle realized an important part of his ambition: to write cheerfully and entertainingly of what he loved, taking the most determinedly *personal* view of things, the more readily as it ran counter to accepted platitudes. His facts, his anecdotes, the very structure of his dissertations on music and painting were unashamedly second-hand; but his views, his tone, his style were boldly his own. He praised Mozart to the skies, made cheerful hash of the prevailing Winckelmannian esthetic of timeless Beauty, steeped his account of the Italian cities in perilously free political talk. His books paid the price of such daring, remaining largely unsold, though they earned him the friendship of those *happy few* for whom the second volume on painting was already inscribed.

Politically, this period of disengagement, reflection on the Italian scene, first-hand observation of the underground struggle against the police state of a foreign occupying power brought his liberal views up to date in an international perspective. Removed from the temptation of office-seeking, he could view with unclouded lucidity the situation in France, where a ghastly regime of émigré politicians was trying to force a return to old rules for the playing of a new game. The calculated futility of Italian political life made painfully clear, moreover, the ugly game by which a nation is kept powerless and fragmented through the vilification and active persecution of its élite. His contacts with the *carbonaro* movement, which were to lead to his eventual expulsion by the Austrian police, cemented the conviction that to love one's country and seek its freedom was the modern analogue of that medieval chivalry the nineteenth century so yearned to disinter. A model was born of *the aristocratic libertarian,* in which both sides of his nature could equally rejoice.

Finally Milan bestowed upon him at this time its headiest and most devastating gift: the great and unrequited love of his life. Not much is known of the exact nature of his relationship to Mathilda Viscontini Dembowski. He loved her to the point of timidity; she never disclosed whether she loved him in return. Fearing the breath of scandal, she first reduced the frequency of his visits, then banished him from her presence altogether. His journal, where one can find every move in his long and bootless "campaign" against Countess Daru plotted in agonized detail, is utterly silent on this decisive crisis of his life, in keeping with his lifelong belief that to write of what truly touches the heart is a desecration. Ample testimony of the depth to which he had been moved comes to us through the pages of *De l'Amour,* the veiled account of his passion in the form of a treatise on love published soon after his return to Paris (1822), and in *The Memoirs of an Egotist* where a decade later he wrote that the mainspring of his conduct in the ensuing years had been to keep any suspicion of his unhappy love affair from the obtuse derision of his friends. It lingered on, finally, in the strangely affecting mixture of pride and gentleness, unaffected gaiety and tender melancholy that characterize the heroines of his greatest novels—Mme de Rênal, Mme de Chasteller, Clelia Conti—all drawn from that tragic model.

Yet return to Paris he did, in 1821, wrapped in thoughts of suicide. His father had died meantime, in 1819, leaving him next to nothing to live on—for that unfortunate parent had managed to combine crassness with mismanagement (or so it seemed to his indignant heir), shattering after half a lifetime of short rations the expectations of ample well-being he had allowed to take root in young Beyle's mind. The modest dream of an independent existence in Paris on six thousand francs per annum had to give way before the necessity of earning at least part of his living. Three British periodicals, the *Paris Monthly Review,* the *London Magazine,* the *Athenaeum,* of which he became a regular collaborator, provided him with the most nearly painless way of meeting that necessity, a way that incidentally afforded him a forum and an audience. He settled down to a routine of café dining and salon going, no longer in the shadow of the Daru clan, though still attached to friends from his native province, such as Countess Beugnot, Baron de Mareste, Count d'Argout. In the salons of Destutt de Tracy (his intellectual mentor), of Etienne Delécluze, of Dr. Edwards he rubbed elbows with the celebrities of the day, acquiring a solid and undeserved reputation of cynicism by his militant wit in the service of unfashionable ideas.* Two short stays in England, a stormy liaison with Countess Curial (which superseded, though it did not obliterate, the agony of the break with Métilde, as he called his now dead love[1]), a blow struck in the battle of French Romanticism, namely *Racine and Shakespeare* (1823, 1825), mark this decade which saw his first, unapplauded venture into the genre that was to give him fame, *Armance* (1827).

The July revolution in Paris having set Louis-Philippe on the throne, Beyle was named consul in Trieste (though Austrian objections to this *carbonaro* sympathizer forced a change to the far meaner post at Civita-Vecchia, in the Papal States). At 47 he proposed, and was refused by the guardian of the beautiful young Giulia Rinieri, who gave herself to him in love. And that same year *The Red and the Black,* begun in 1829, saw the light of day in Paris, as its author in the month of November sailed to Trieste. *Visse, scrisse, amò . . . .*

Amid the petty vexations of his administrative career, caught between local intrigue and pressure from the home office, the French consul at Civita-Vecchia managed to pursue, in that last decade of his life, at a feverish pace, the life of the pen and of the heart. Giulia Rinieri, Countess Cini, Countess Curial, Mme Jules Gaultier, an anonymous Roman lady he called in his journals Earline—"his laste *(sic)* romance"—give witness in turn to the enduringly youthful effervescence of a heart that knew no greater happiness than the tumultuous course of imperfectly reciprocated passion. And a stream of writings, many of them penned during his frequent and prolonged leaves of absence from his post, marks the full release of his creative genius, in the direct exploitation of his feelings and experience both in fiction and in autobiographical memoirs (destined for the public of 1900). *Memoirs of an Egotist* (1832) and *The Life of Henry*

Brulard (1835) were undertaken in these years, as well as a host of fragmentary and autobiographical sketches. The tales which were to be collected into the two volumes of the *Italian Chronicles* (1855) appeared for the most part in the *Revue des Deux-Mondes* and the *Revue de Paris* between 1829 and 1839; a last travel account, *Memoirs of a Tourist,* came out in two volumes in 1838; there were, in addition, several novellas, a couple of which, *Mina de Vanghel* (1830) and *Feder* (1839), might in finished form have ended up short novels; three unfinished novels that rank among his undoubted masterpieces: *The Rose and the Green* (1837), *Lamiel* (1840), *Lucien Leuwen* (1834); finally, dashed off at feverish pace in two months' time, *The Charterhouse of Parma* (1839). Quite a haul, though no man not yet in his fifties need draw too easy solace from this extraordinary bout of productivity, who does not take thought that nearly a lifetime of literary apprenticeship had by then elapsed, under the stern injunction: *"Write two hours a day—genius or no"!*

Little remains to be told. In 1842, Consul Beyle, recovering in Paris from a bout of apoplexy that had felled him in March of the previous year, had been two weeks at work on a revision of his *Italian Chronicles* when apoplexy struck again in a Paris street. He died, without having recovered consciousness, that death *repentinam inopinatamque* (sudden and unforeseen) which Cæsar recommended, and he himself had wished for. This was on March 23, 1842, a year and a week after his first attack.

II *Portrait of the Artist*

The facts of this account, though they do not pertain exclusively to the public side of the life of Henri Beyle—the character of a writer's love affairs is not easily dissociated from his biography—do yield a portrait of a somewhat unusual man of letters: a first *mask,* the one most directly perceived by his contemporaries, of a somewhat marginal though undoubtedly striking figure—Sainte-Beuve's hussar of literature. Stendhal cavalry man is of course neither quite borne out nor unequivocally belied by the foregoing biographical sketch. He *did* see fire on horseback, though his time as a line officer was mostly spent on sick leave, and his military experience was largely confined to the services of supply (none too softly, just the same, in the harrowing retreat from Moscow). It remains true that he spent his life in military and diplomatic service, the former in a relatively high administrative capacity. The Napoleonic legend was to him first-hand experience, and his sentiments toward the great man considerably more ambivalent, in consequence, than those of his literary peers. The heroic tide had served him well: it opened the windows of cosmopolitan experience, in Italy and Germany, upon his French heritage—which appeared to him severely shrunk, a just prey to the ridicule which alone could pierce its smugness. It had delivered to him as well that precious antidote to romantic embroidery: the knowledge of the crassness, the bungling, the bellowing self-importance and habitual cowardice that form the underside of the heroic life. Finally, a lifetime of service to the French State had given him experience in the backstage realities of political life, teaching him that under whatever rules, quite unfailingly the same sordid game is being played.

Yet the self that stands revealed in the autobiographical memoirs is little touched, nonetheless, by politics or ambition. Love and hate—total espousal, utter rejection—throw up into strong relief the features of that inner landscape, which remained largely unknown even to his intimate contemporaries, but lives for us with utmost vividness in the pages of *Henry Brulard* and *Souvenirs d'égotisme.* The introspective glance of the fifty-two-year-old memorialist makes his childhood stand out with the schematic sharpness of a pre-Freudian scenario: *I was in love with my mother—and came to love all that she stood for. She was taken from me in my seventh year: "that is when I began to speak ill of* God,"[2] *and came to hate my father—and all that* he *stood for.*

Fond as he was of repeating that what he wrote as paradox in 1835 would be regarded as hardly worth stating in 1935, Stendhal could not possibly have foreseen the bland orthodoxy that was to descend upon this defiant Genesis in the age of Freud, nor could he have accepted without pain that his hard-won lucidity should be accorded the honors of quaint anticipation. Let us grant him the distinction, in any event, of having taken his stand against the prevailing winds of sentimentality and pomposity on the rock bottom of the experienced self: *I may be a monster (though I suspect not), but I am that I am.* Rousseau, whose *Confessions* were one of the source books of his own growing up—as they were to be for Julien Sorel—had set the pattern for the defiant claims of the deviant self; but Rousseau had sought refuge in moral justification. Stendhal was content to be *other* tauntingly. He had loved his mother physically: he had wanted to cover her with kisses, "and that there be no clothes."[3] He lashes the imagined reader of his own time, the shocked admirer of Chateaubriand or follower of Guizot, with the joyful monstrosity of such a breaker of taboos, whom physical necessity alone restrained from incestuous consummation: "It was with me as far as the physical side of love went, as it would be with Caesar, if he were to return to this world, for the use of guns and small arms: I should have learned fast, it would have made no difference in my basic line of attack."[4] To paraphrase a celebrated twentieth-century homily, it is as if Stendhal proclaimed: "We must imagine Œdipus to have been happy!" A complex neither duly repressed nor tearfully assuaged (or, in analysis, quaveringly defused) but smilingly flaunted may rate high marks for originality even in this age of discarded inhibitions! It represents, in any event, midway between scientific observation and romantic self-advertisement, the stance that is uniquely Stendhal's, of turning the tables on the world, raising the shocking standard of private happiness over the dismantled Bastille of order and conformity, careerism and servility.

What after all is the full range of implications of that fundamental choice? "Daydreaming," he wrote, "I have preferred over all things else."[5] His mother's early death released her world into the security of a dream—inaccessible to the vulgar, unimperiled by sensuality. There was little risk in his incestuous pose, under the circumstances; and everything to gain from an absolute claim to happiness, when happiness had been so absolutely withdrawn. A sensuous heaven existed, of which the dream, rekindled by Ariosto, *La Nouvelle Héloïse,* and Shakespeare's comedies, proclaimed that it was to be found in the love of woman; a heaven over which the departed mother presided as a hallowing, permissive shade.

She had been a gay and spirited woman, and love, for him, though tinged with the tender melancholy of Mozart and Correggio, was essentially radiant and joyful, an apparition beyond the reach and sight of the scoffers and the plodders, vouchsafed to none other than the unsuspecting knight Parsifal.

The world of the mother reached beyond the charmed circle of dreams and dream-begotten tales of Tasso, Ariosto, Cervantes, Shakespeare, Fielding, and Rousseau. The maternal clan, a benevolent trinity made up of the grandfather, Dr. Henri Gagnon, the dashing young uncle Romain Gagnon, and a great-aunt, Elisabeth Gagnon, successfully extended the mother's tutelary shade into the daylight world of living affections and practical decisions. His grandfather's house, ample, well-lit, whose well-stocked library was watched over by a bust of Voltaire, provided daily refuge from the cramped and gloomy quarters presided over by his hated aunt Séraphie. A figure of elegance, of learning worn with easy grace, the town physician—and its leader in cultural affairs—Henri Gagnon stamped the age of Enlightenment, where he had his spiritual being, with a decisively affirmative imprint in his grandson's eyes. Though Stendhal never learned to share the older man's worship of Voltaire (who early and late repelled him by his want of feeling) the thought and taste of the eighteenth century were to operate the happiest conjunction with his impetuously romantic preference for the dreamily remote and the wildly impractical. Science—a science of the mind that would make one master of one's own destiny and a power among men, by disentangling one's own motives as readily as theirs—he later sought to acquire from such disciples of Helvetius and Condillac as Cabanis and Destutt de Tracy, the masters of the Ideology school. All ideas are traceable to sensations, all sensations bear witness to a physical cause; patience and attentive observation therefore must eventually yield a physiology of motivation wherewith to account for all mental phenomena. The assumptions were crude, but to this largely self-taught adolescent the eighteenth-century quest for human control of human destiny seemed to yield a key to the human heart which no future Molière could afford to neglect.

These thoughts were not to assail him before his stay in Paris in 1805, when Stendhal's lifelong *tic* of rigorous deduction in matters of the heart was to acquire, in the writings of the Ideologues, its theoretical foundations. Back in Grenoble, at the newly founded Ecole centrale—joint offspring of the young Republic and of Dr. Gagnon's civic-mindedness—young Henri Beyle made a more immediate and equally liberating application of the intellectual world of his grandfather: a fervent study of mathematics, as the antidote to a world of lies and superstitions. How utterly Stendhalian that this strange creed should have worked, that love in this case engendered proficiency, and proficiency crowned by a prize led to freedom in Paris, on the wings of a dream of Ecole polytechnique which seems to have turned more sober parental heads as effectively as it did Henri's own!

Romain Gagnon played a significant supporting role in this elaboration of an eighteenth-century outlook, where a dangerously Wertherian temperament might otherwise have evolved. This charming and accomplished ladies' man, whose wardrobe reflected the solicitude of his grateful mistresses, gave the ungainly youth a sense of that erotic mastery which forms an important side of eighteenth-century preoccupations. That women were not solely to be dreamed of, but that—given certain quite simple prescriptions—they could also be conquered and possessed, was heady news for the boy, whose fiery imaginings so drastically outstripped his *savoir faire.* To be seductive, better still to sweep elegant and charming women off their feet in the manner of Don Juan was to be an essential in young Beyle's life plan; and that there was somewhere an infallible *technique* to that end became his lifelong conviction—a conviction reinforced on his arrival in Paris by the encounter with his cousin Martial Daru. Martial picked up where Uncle Romain had left off, introducing the adolescent into the world of actresses, instructing him by example in the handling, at least, of *approachable* women. For while Henri Beyle somewhat ruefully rated himself as the imperial functionary who had had the fewest women, Martial, he thought, led the honor list, pointing, as the uncle had done, the way to that worldly success which his quite imperfectly accomplished disciple held alone desirable. Stendhal could have made his own the words of his master Rousseau: *I have loved women too well to have been successful with them.* But though he took pride in the dream that made him unworldly, his eighteenth-century heritage, both scientific and practical, insisted on the having as well as the dreaming. A will to mastery flourished side by side with the habitual floundering of helpless love. It is this ambivalence, together with his consciousness that the Don Juan side of him was a face-saving myth, easily overwhelmed by the lovably inept Rousseau figure, that gives his views of himself—and of the heroes created in his image—the fascination of an inner dialectic.

His great-aunt Elisabeth contributed a decisively asymmetric ingredient to this Enlightenment brew. To her he ascribed what in *Henry Brulard* he called the Spanish side of his makeup—his *espagnolisme.* Her lofty integrity, her passionate regard for all that exhibited the grander side of human nature, her silent contempt for what was low found a ready echo in the admirer of Tasso and would-be doer of chivalric deeds. Their common yearning for the noble and the uncompromising, their common worship of honor merged in a shared taste for the theater of Corneille. A kind of innocence bound these two, the child and the old maid, together. In the tribunal of the grown man's conscience Great-aunt Elisabeth stood guard over the finer impulses of his nature. As the one feminine surrogate of the mother's presence, she refined still further the quality of distance and height—distance uncrossable by mortals, height unscalable by the unblest—which death had bestowed on *das ewig Weibliche.* Arduousness, or at any rate the kind of purity required of a hero, and which melts obstacles and exorcises danger in the very onslaught that carries him into the thick of it, came to enshrine the figure of bliss, otherwise wrapped in *douce volupté,* that the departed Henriette Gagnon had left so fresh, so *alive,* so unforbiddingly smiling in her little boy's heart.

From these blessed heights the descent to the flatlands which were the abode of the father was steep and breathtaking. The unhappy Chérubin Beyle was doomed never to gain his son's affection or even understanding. That reserved, hard-working, conscientious family man had wasted his youth in caring for ten sisters to be provided for. He had the misfortune to lose his charming and youthful wife relatively early in their marriage. The Republic broke his career in the magistracy, and snuffed out his expectations of wealth by a change in the laws of inheritance. Land speculation in which he engaged to recoup his losses left him further impoverished. Failure never did endear a father to his son, much less so when it clips his wings, as he seeks to rise clear of its potential gloom. A kind of gloomy pride was indeed the noxious mixture young Beyle felt he had been made to breathe at home: injured prospects grafted on morose gentility engendered *ennui* in his mentors, and the child paid for it, as he thought, in that regime of sheltered repressiveness and half-pampered solitude that is too often called childhood in the French middle class.

Money early and late fueled the son's dislike of his father. The cramped, nay-saying household of the father stood in painful contrast to the large, fashionable, brilliant house of the well-to-do and respected Dr. Gagnon. Money was clearly the center of the father's unhappy preoccupations, while the subject was deemed too low to be mentioned in the Gagnon circle. Hence the grubby side of existence became unalterably associated in young Beyle's mind with the figure of the miserly provider, who promised wealth and high standing but grudgingly disbursed a pittance. And it only came as further humiliation that once in the grave the miser was revealed to have been a pauper. Disinterestedness became the religion of the son whose father had neither soared above pelf, nor properly battened on it. He was to plume himself repeatedly in his memoirs and sketches on having turned down a post worth millions, which Count Beugnot had offered him in the early days of the Restoration: he did not seek to resemble his father, even to outdo him and show him up at his own game.

Failure was to be the least of his father's sins, however. On the death of the mother an infernal trinity had been established, opposed to and symmetrical with the celestial Gagnon triad, through the fatal alliance his father contracted with God and Aunt Séraphie—the former represented by the dismal Abbé Raillane. Grief made his father somber, and that chilling mood, so brutally contrasting with the mother's youthful gaiety, was heightened and confirmed by his choice of Henriette's younger sister Séraphie to take over the household. She was shrill, repressive, and appeared to the boy to hold no love for him. Whether, as he later theorized, she had her eye on marriage with the widower, is quite immaterial; in the mythology of his childhood set down in the last decade of his life, she fully played the role of the stepmother, the Fury risen from religion's hell to dispossess the mother "taken away" by God.

For it was in this manner that religion entered his life, locked in unholy alliance with the hateful gloomy father and the bride of his choice. What looked to the child like murder marked that entry. "This comes of God, my friend:" words of conventional piety spoken as Christian solace by Abbé Rey to his bereaved father, they rang with awesome literalness in Henri's ears. Henceforth he "began to speak ill of *God.*"[6] The father had turned to God, and these two murderers of the mother had called in Aunt Séraphie to take her place. The three of them (God being represented by the chill and untidy tutor Abbé Raillane) then proceeded, in the name of love, of their concern for his well-being, *for his own good,* to upbraid and instruct and rebuke and confine the ungrateful child. "It was with me . . . as with the nations of Europe today," he wrote in 1835, "my tyrants always spoke to me in the gentlest tones of the most tender solicitude, and religion was their staunchest ally." *(OI, H. Brulard,* 85)

The Revolution reverberated upon this puny scene in most unexpected fashion. The embattled child felt himself, by the grace of History, become one with a vast and momentous uprising. Tyrants were on the run while the people's chains were falling from them; the once hectoring priests were now themselves persecuted: his father's world was shattered, and his father himself went into hiding and even found himself (for a brief spell) in jail. The little boy openly exulted at his elders' dismay: he made common cause with the Republic, he even ran off one night to join a meeting of the local Jacobin club—only to discover his lifelong inability to stand at close quarters the speech, the looks, the manners of *the rabble* which, as *the people,* he sincerely loved from afar.

Stendhal thus came by his republican convictions in a way that rooted them in the depths of his being. The Revolution was the embodiment of the Enlightenment faith in practical reason, in man's ability to throw off the shackles of the past and see through the lies of those who would keep him unfree. That faith in light had triumphed over the dark, murderous, deceptive faith of the priests: it had toppled both the throne of oppression and the altar of lies, giving promise that never again need men read their whole fate in the accident of birth. To be a republican was for Stendhal to be a man of the present, to see things as they are, for no amount of political tinkering could turn back the clock: the Revolution had spoken words in the ears of mankind which too clearly appealed to every man's self-interest ever to be wholly undone. This knowledge merged with his very genuine sympathy for the common people (the oppressed little boy in him still saw their cause as his) in which his almost feminine sensibility had its part (Julien Sorel would have to fight back his tears when the pauper's song was silenced for the convenience of the poorhouse director's dinner guests!) His allegiance was to remain divided, however, between love of cause and happiness. The latter ideal was to be transcendent. In the clash between head and heart, heart won out in life as it would in the novels, and the Revolution gained a lover, though it never acquired a fighter or even a party faithful.

Paris was to play an important role in sidetracking young Beyle from the love of homeland, inseparable from revolutionary fervor, in the days when the place in men's hearts left open by the fall of the king had been filled by the idea of the Nation. The heartless sophistication of the capital suited him no better than had the money-grubbing simplicities of Grenoble. In that arid landscape he came to regret the sight of his native mountains, though homesickness was certainly far from his thoughts. His disappointment with Paris turned rather into a heightened sense of his own apartness, which would today have found a name: alienation. The French mentality began to stand out in his eyes as something foreign and objectionable. Italy, which he was to reach by way of Rousseau country in a fever of literary and artistic exaltation, by presenting him with the true homeland of his soul, the landscape of happiness that had beckoned to him through books and flights of private fancy ever since the death of his mother—Italy was to crystallize his un-French view of the French, providing the enchanting setting in which the ugly duckling at last could grow into a swan.

Italy turned Beyle into Stendhal. It assured him of his tastes, revealed to him his own temperament, and it justified his dream world by the example of a gifted and attractive nation devoted unabashedly to the intensest enjoyment of life. In Italy he discovered music. His love of the theater (sparked by successive infatuations with several actresses) merged with it in the Italian cult of the opera. He found religion there stripped of moral pretense and revered as directly and unthinkingly as had been the gods of old. He found a way of life that differed radically from what he had known (and hated), that bubbled with immediacy and vitality (he was to call it *energy*), and that seemed to offer a direct link with the simpler and more admirable world of medieval and Renaissance achievement. He was instructed, in a word, in that primacy of manners to which, in line with his masters Helvetius and Montesquieu, he traced all that is significant in the works of men. The novels of his maturity were to be the glorious harvest of that sense of national difference gleaned in the cosmopolitan setting of his experience—Paris, Milan, Leipzig, Moscow.

Italy, as we have seen, was to bring him also that taste of passionate love—and of its wounds—that alone, for this particular practitioner of *la chasse au bonheur,* gave to life its savor. No vain concern for what the neighbors thought came to blunt the fine edge of passion in that blessed land: a man could here, without fear of ridicule, let himself be overwhelmed by the fullness of his feelings—*nature,* not *art,* was mistress of this battlefield. In his long-delayed "conquest" of Angela Pietragrua Stendhal experienced to the full the theatricality that made a love affair into an all-absorbing, life-draining experience, in which duplicity itself wore a mask of intensity quite undreamt of in tamer climes. Angela, her lusty faithlessness discovered at last, pursued him to the door on her knees: faintly comical? operatic? without a doubt; but more *real,* heartfelt, alive than the months of peck-and-pout coquetry in Adèle Rebuffel's salon. And when he came to love Métilde, when the shyness of his teens overcame the retired Napoleonic officer in his late thirties, when he learned to tremble in her presence and lose countenance at the glimpse of a shade behind her curtains, he experienced to the full the tragic reality of a feeling none would laugh at in a land that gave feeling full rein—in bitterness no less readily than in delight.

The face of Consul Beyle, as we have seen, was a mask that concealed as much as it revealed. The work of the memorialist Stendhal allowed to come into view a second mask, that of Henry Brulard, torn between love of glory and a dreamer's ineptitude, Werther and Don Juan, republican rectitude and lover's abandon. This second self engendered a third. On his return to Paris from heartbreak in Milan his overwhelming object, he recalls in *Souvenirs d'Egotisme,* was *not to be seen through ("ne pas être deviné")*. The existence of an infinitely vulnerable dreamer beneath the façade of reasonable social and professional competence made it imperative to resort to a strategy of masks to keep the truth, the laughable truth, unguessed at · in the land of scoffers. Hence the Stendhal of contemporary accounts, the impenitent atheist of Mérimée's memoir "H. B." and the fire-eating cavalry officer who shocked mild Destutt de Tracy and his guests with a dragooning solution to the émigré problem, the hussar of literature depicted by Sainte-Beuve, who entered the battle of Romanticism with a whiff of grapeshot entitled *Racine and Shakespeare,* in which he haughtily proclaimed that to be Romantic was nothing more than to be of one's own blessed post-revolutionary time, relegating the Neo-Classicists to the ultramontane dump heap of reactionary politics.

A protective pose of cynicism allied itself in him with two of the basic strands in his nature: the secretiveness prized and cultivated in the men of the · Dauphiné—a sly, closemouthed, *deep* lot—which his beleaguered childhood in "the enemy camp" did nothing to curtail; and his Don Juan ideologue belief that success in love was largely a matter of tactics, that the prize invariably would go to the cooler head. This mixture of eighteenth-century pragmatism and temperamental reserve flowered in a harvest of steely aphorisms that established Monsieur de Stendhal's hard-bitten military stance in matters of sentiment and insured that the provocative insulating layer of cynicism in his novels would be taken at face value. Add to this recipe the half-playful, half-justified cloak-and-dagger game by which he sought to outwit the Austrian police in his correspondence and, in his journals, to blunt the indiscretion of a possible intruder (through bizarre spellings, enigmatic initials, false parentheses, and a veritable cloud of fanciful pseudonyms for himself, his friends, and the women he loved*), and we have the outline of the elaborate strategy of deception by which the writer, like some latter-day Penelope, unwove by night what he took equal pains to set before others by day.

It is amid such conflicting eddies of revelation and concealment that the novels were born. A casual confrontation of the three great novels—*The Red and the Black, Lucien Leuwen, The Charterhouse of*

Parma—with the autobiographical writings leaves no doubt in anyone's mind that the novels constitute, in part, a transposed, idealized recreation of the author's self-image. Few great novels have managed to skirt the treacherous bogs of simple wish-fulfillment so heedlessly, and with such perfect impunity. The secret of that impunity may well lie in the complex interplay of tenderness and irony that marks the author's approach to the fragile and indomitable impersonations of his many-layered younger self. But perhaps the deeper truth concerning the unalterable freshness of his masterpieces is to be found in the enduring youthfulness of the author himself, recorded for us in the last of his autobiographical writings, with which it may be fitting to close this account of the man behind the masks.

Among Stendhal's papers was found a short document entitled "The Privileges of April 10, 1840"—dating therefore from his fifty-seventh and next-to-last year on earth. This cheerful fantasy is made up of 23 articles, of which the following give a fair sample, and is headed: "GOD* hands me the following warrant":

First Article

Never any serious pain, into advanced old age; then, not pain, but death by apoplexy, in bed, during sleep. . . .

In any one year no more than three days of upsets. The body, and what comes out of it, free of smell.

Art. 3

The *mentula,* like the index finger in hardness and motion, and this at will. In shape, two inches more than the article in question, same thickness. But pleasure through the *mentula,* no more than twice a week.

Twenty times a year the privileged shall be able to change into whomever he chooses, provided that person exists. . . .

Art. 4

Wearing a ring on his finger and squeezing it tight while looking at a woman, she will fall passionately in love with the privileged as did Héloise with Abelard. If the ring is touched with a little saliva the woman looked at will become just a tender and devoted friend. . . . Hatred will turn to benevolence, by looking at the hating person while rubbing the ring worn on the finger.

Art. 6

Miracles in the eyes of those who don't know him: the privileged will wear the face of General Debelle, who died in Santo Domingo, completely without blemish. He'll play faultlessly at wisk *(sic),* écarté, billiards, chess, but won't ever win more than 100 francs. He'll shoot pistols, ride horseback, fence to perfection.

Art. 9

Every day, at two in the morning, the privileged will find in his pocket a gold napoleon, plus forty francs' worth of the currency of the country he finds himself in. . . . In the act of striking him or handing him poison assassins will have an acute fit of cholera lasting eight days. The privileged shall be able to curtail these sufferings by saying: I pray that so-and-so's sufferings be turned into lesser sufferings.

Art. 13

The privileged shall be unable to steal; if he tried, his organs would deny him service. He shall be able to kill ten human beings a year; but none to whom he shall have spoken. . . .

Art. 15

The privileged, turning the ring on his finger and saying: I pray that all noxious insects be wiped out; all insects six yards away from the ring in every direction shall be struck dead. . . .

Art. 18

Ten times a year, upon request, the privileged shall be able to reduce by three-quarters the pain of someone he sees; or should this being be on the point of death he could prolong his life for ten days, while reducing the actual pain by three quarters. He shall obtain, upon request, a sudden and painless death for this suffering being.

Art. 20

The privileged shall never be more unhappy than he was from August 1st, 1839 to April 1st, 1840. . . .

Art. 21

Twenty times a year, the privileged shall be able to guess the thoughts of all the persons around him at a distance of twenty paces. One nundred twenty times a year, he shall be able to see what whoever he chooses is doing at the time; there is total exception for the woman he loves best.

There is another exception for dirty and disgusting actions.

Art. 22

The privileged shall earn no money outside his sixty francs a day by means of the privileges enunciated above. One hundred fifty times a year he shall obtain on request that such and such a person forget him, the privileged, altogether.

Art. 23

Ten times a year, the privileged shall be transported to the place he chooses, at the rate of a hundred leagues an hour; during the transfer he shall sleep.

Frederic de STENDHAL.[7]

The whimsicality of the whole notion need not deter us from seeking a meaning in these lines, for it constitutes in itself the chief part of such a meaning. A man of fifty-seven makes up for himself, tongue in cheek, a talisman that supplies all his needs and gratifies all the standard wishes (mind reading, beauty, skill, sex appeal, instant removal to other sites or other selves) and even descends into the specifics of sexual measurement and frequency. Among the needs: freedom from pain, sex, love, money, food (Art. 16) form a descending progression significantly stripped of all cant. Among the wishes: personal good looks, impeccable skill, and generously renewed attire (Art. 5) testify to a lingering unhappiness with his own looks, for which skill and dress were, in his eyes, potent remedies. Fleas, lice, bedbugs gravely enumerated in Article 15 (on extermination) add a touch of comedy to an already smiling production, addressed to an audience of one, let us remember. But a characteristic gentleness and delicacy surround even these quite free, quite private, quite uncensored lucubrations: the privileged seeks passionate love and tender friendship, and only wishes to dissolve hatred—not return it. True, he seeks the privilege of killing ten men a year if need be (a concession to his old warrior pose and most likely a *political* wish, as the sequel confirms), but introduces the significant condition that they must not be even remote personal acquaintances—which confirms the rather abstract quality of his blood-thirstiness. This exception is made up for by the admirable Article 18, devoted entirely to the relief of the sufferings of others (in the self-same ratio of ten a year). And a note of delicacy emerges miraculously in full magic fantasizing, in Article 21, where mind-reading privileges stop abruptly where the beloved is concerned.

In sum, to the mystery of self—the "who am I?" of Stendhal's every reflection upon himself—there corresponds in the very awareness of the mystery, taken together with the lifelong search for an answer, the delineation of a kind of character—tender, amused, ironic, tough-minded, bewildered and yet quite self-assured, probing and witty, sharp and also incorrigibly starry-eyed. He took into the grave with him at fifty-nine a little boy who had never stopped making faces in the mirror. Elevated feelings, self-forgetful love, tender music, a gentle Lombardy landscape remained to the last a chosen dream homeland bequeathed to the older man by the child who would not give up his hold on the mother's loving shade. Unlike Gide, who said that in him there lived a little boy accompanied by a Protestant pastor who bored him, Stendhal's little boy found in his aging self an indulgent but wary mentor, who shared his dream but could smile at himself for doing so, and never forgot to let wit stand guard upon delight, lest the scoffers get the scent of such tender prey.

In the end, we must let Stendhal write his own epitaph.[8] Its one lie points to a deeper truth; the progression speaks for itself; the blending of music, love, and letters in final homage reveals that deepest self that flourished above all on passionate affirmation.

ERRICO BEYLE
MILANESE
Visse, Scrisse, Amò
QUEST' ANIMA
ADORAVA
CIMAROSA, MOZART E SHAKESPEARE
MORI DI ANNI . . . .
IL . . . . 18 . .

* It is from this period of his life that we can date Stendhal's lifelong friendship with Prosper Mérimée. The author of *Carmen* penned the memoir "H.B.", in fact, which in 1850 was to give the world its first inkling of the original and complex personality it had lost in Henri Beyle.

* Alberthe de Rubempré, who lived on Blue Street, was called Mme Azur; Countess Clementine Curial became Menti; his friend Joseph Lingay, who had served under the Duke Decazes (casa = Italian for house), is invariably referred to as Maisonnette (little house). As to Stendhal himself, this list is just a sample: Brulard, Mocenigo, Banti, Dominique, chef de bataillon Coste, 2d Ltnt. Lecœur, Darlincourt, Smith & Co., Cotonet, César Bombet, etc. . . .

* That name almost invariably appears in English in the journals, in mixed playfulness and perhaps a reluctance to leave the name of the Lord to those who truly profane it–His faithful.

CHAPTER 1

The Pistol Shot

"POLITICS in a work of imagination is like a pistol shot in a concert." Stendhal liked the image, and used it in several novels. What he liked about it most, I suppose, is that it is not true. Far from jarring our senses, politics is the stuff of the Stendhalian novel: we could no more imagine Julien Sorel indifferent to Bonaparte than Fabrizio absent from Waterloo. Clearly this is one of the statements by which a major writer distinguishes his work from what passes for literature in the hands of lesser practioners, as Cervantes nailed the knightly romances on the lance point of the knight of his imagination. *The Red and the Black, Lucien Leuwen, The Charterhouse of Parma*—each represents a precise moment in the political unfolding of post-revolutionary Europe, each measures itself in its hero by the distance he traveled or the strength he drew from the French Revolution, and its comet's tail Napoleon—each is the embodiment of a particular political betrayal. The peculiar genius of French classical drama for a reciprocal confrontation of private passion and public interest (Racine presses a crown on Phaedra's brow as she staggers between incest and suicide) seems to be reborn in these masterpieces of the Romantic age. The intensely private love that burns at the center of each of these novels burns so bright by reason of the conflict of loyalties it evokes, for hero and heroine as invariably belong to enemy worlds of class and political warfare as did Romeo and Juliet to the warring clans of Montague and Capulet. In fact, the Stendhalian hero is a hero, in the eyes of the woman whose love redeems and transfigures him, precisely by reason of his will to amount to something, which in the case of each of these outsiders automatically takes on the aspect of a political act. Hence the obligation, if we are to make sense of the Stendhalian world, to take it up first from the standpoint of the particular political arrangements which, in each one of the three great novels, gives it the *gestalt* by which it coheres as a novel and as a world.[1]

I *From Sawmill to Scaffold*

Published in 1830, *The Red and the Black* offers itself as a chronicle of 1830: the claim of the Stendhalian novel could not be more clearly staked out.[2] Julien Sorel's self-imposed assignment could probably be stated thus: how is a gifted young man of the lower classes, during his own lifetime, in fact at the height of his powers, come into what the Revolution had designated as his heritage, in the France of Louis XVIII and Charles X? To allow his answer its full devastating power we must look into the circumstances of its formulation.

Julien was the hated delicate son of a small-town peasant entrepreneur, *le père* Sorel, who with the help of the boy's more robust and brutal brothers had built up a flourishing sawmill enterprise. Born into the meanest circumstances socially, his passionate ambition might very well have taken account of the rising economic power of that same social class, symbolized in the novel by the elder Sorel's successful humiliation of the powerful and wealthy mayor of the town, M. de Rênal, twice beaten down in unsuccessful bargaining sessions with that iron-willed, steely-eyed neighbor. But the slow rise which money insures, without fanfare and with little risk, this almost natural course by which power changes hands with practically no visible upheaval, by a kind of seeping upward, of osmosis, held no charm for the boy. He was to prove it again later on, by turning down his good friend Fouqué's offer of a profitable partnership in the fuel business. Stendhalian will to power has little use for Balzacian means. Julien's childhood had been rescued from sorrow and dreariness by the tales of battle of a retired surgeon-major, a relic of Napoleon's Grand Army. They had instilled a worship of Napoleon, a passionate will to emulate his glory, to rise to the top on wings of heroism. Frail, bookish, handsome, intense Julien Sorel clutched to his bosom the two Testaments of his covenant with greatness—the victory bulletins of the Grand Army and Rousseau's *Confessions*—and plotted in secret his lonely charge against the world of men.

It would certainly be farfetched to view this determination—so far—as political. Julien was no more to be a Bonapartist than had been Stendhal himself, who had served under the great man, chafed under his authoritarian ways, taken due note of the self-made Emperor's haste to have himself a nobility and a court of his own. Napoleon offered an example, not a political label; an example of the promise of the Revolution fulfilled extravagantly in the career of a commoner, who managed in a decade to shake every throne in Europe, tossing vacant crowns to his next-of-kin, taking on the world, as it were, single-handed—and, *in the end,* leaving it, never to be quite the same again. A commoner could aspire to do all that nature and will fitted him for: Napoleon merely pointed to the sky as the limit. The portrait of Napoleon that Julien secreted under his mattress, and that Mme de Rênal could only surmise with chagrin to be that of a woman, stood, therefore, in spite of the political risk he incurred, not so much for a political decision as for a personal choice: the choice of himself as the Napoleon of *his* age. Like the heroes of Plutarch for Rousseau or Montaigne, Napoleon had quite simply exemplary value for Julien. He stood before him as one who had given the world his full measure as a man, challenging the boy to do the same. The portrait of Napoleon was in that sense the portrait of himself—of the self to which every day of his short life he was to hold that life to account.

Hence it is in the choice of *how* he was to be the Napoleon of his age that the full political implications of his determination came to the fore. Deliberately understated, that choice of the black cassock of Restoration ambition over the red coat of Napoleonic heroism is the boldest stroke of the book. Julien's dream of greatness transcended its romantic origins, the ego's wish for instant transfiguration on the stirrups of military glory. Heroically, he sacrificed heroism on the altar of reality. And reality, Restoration political reality, was revealed to him when he saw an honest judge render a series of iniquitous decisions—involving tiny sums—against readers of the *Constitutionnel,* the opposition Liberal paper. This judge has been embroiled in a feud with "the young curate who was rumored to be the spy of the Congregation" (the *Opus Dei* of the day), this in the time that a splendid new church was being built in Verrières (the locale of the first and last chapters of the novel). The judge's shameful capitulation, the sight of four marble columns in a town little given to luxury spoke eloquently of the new dawn of ecclesiastical power. Julien, under the tutelage of the honest vicar Chélan, began to commit the Latin New Testament to memory.

To the question: how is a gifted young peasant to rise under Charles X, the answer is given—by beating them at their own game. Julien Sorel was to be hired by M. de Rênal as the tutor of his children, in deference to the appearances this noble personage felt called upon to maintain—as the head of the local political establishment. This elevation the carpenter's son owed to the prodigious memory that allowed him to repeat verbatim any passage of the Latin Scriptures, with no more concern for their meaning than he found in his dazzled bumpkin audience. The stunt camouflaged his dangerous intellectual powers, while the gaze that saw through the fog of official pieties was reverently lowered in mock submission.

The much-vexed question of Julien Sorel's hypocrisy, in other words, reduces to the kind of tactical breakthrough he would himself, as a reader of Napoleon's victory bulletins,[3] have preferred to call it. The society upon which he was launching his lonely assault had mobilized a faith in which it did not believe, to maintain in subjection to a ruling clique of émigrés a nation that had received the heady gospel of freedom and equality, and whose commoner sons were being held back from claiming their rightful place by empty slogans (HATRED OF THE UNGODLY—PERPETUAL ADORATION OF GOD [126]) and ultramontane machinations. To conquer without an army, he had simply to neutralize the enemy by seeming to share his assumptions. By playing more royalist than the king, he might just slip unnoticed into the heart of the regime: the Church militant. Quoting scripture to his masters, he read them the lesson by which they would have kept him in his place. The odds now came out even: the Big Lie was rendered harmless to one who dared to lie twice.

The New Testament kept them off his scent: Horace established him as an equal. In the days of his near immolation, at the Besançon seminary, acquaintance with that pagan ornament of mandarin culture had earned him low marks on his examinations and the amused admiration of the local bishop. Later on in Paris it gave him a chance to shine at the table of the Marquis de La Mole ("Apparently these people don't know any other author" [258]). Once having passed the hurdle of blind obedience to what the society deemed safe for its servants to know, he could safely take on the protective coloration of the higher culture.

His elevation to that trusted proximity to the ruling circles had been paved by conquest, instantly atoned for by retraction and submission. No sooner had Julien won acceptance as a member of the Rênal household—at the very center of small-town social and political power—where his position had all the bittersweet ambiguousness of social mutation (his black suit was his livery, but he ate with the masters[4]), than he felt it *his duty* to "conquer" the obviously solicitous Mme de Rênal. Ignorant of love and almost totally unacquainted with women, he set himself the harrowing task, peasant child in cleric's clothes that he was, to climb into the bed of the first lady he had ever come to know. Heroic summonses to battle emboldened him to take, then to hold, her hand under cover of darkness in the evening conversations with the lady and her friend, under the linden of the Vergy country house garden. An ultimatum to himself dragged him to her room half-dead with apprehension, only to collapse in her lap, at two in the morning, and to receive, in the numbness of recent shock, the prize he had striven for so heroically.[5]

The conquest of Mme de Rênal plotted in anger and pride, as an episode in the class warfare that had to be waged and won before the seats of power could come within his reach, turned out to be a victory of a magnitude he could not have suspected. It brought with it, to be sure, immediate satisfactions of pride and male vanity, and it initiated him into a world of sensual delight, of trust, of intimacy with another that had been a dead letter for him, a refugee from peasant grossness and violence[6] living in the cold barracks of his secret dreams. But in terms of his long-range objectives, it had, more importantly, lifted him at a stroke up to the level of his masters: Mme de Rênal had taught him both the fine points of worldly knowledge and the detailed backstage maneuvers that would allow him to cut a figure in the society he sought to master, capping her instructions with the gift of a caper on horseback and in uniform, as a member of the honor guard put up by the town of Verrières for the reception of a king.

This early high point of his career, a kind of festive grand rehearsal for the role which secretly he wished to play, also marked the necessity for orderly retreat. The privilege of membership in the honor guard, for which Liberal ladies had abjectly courted the mayor's wife in their husbands' name, had not devolved unnoticed upon the peasant lad in the Rênals' employ. An anonymous letter soon alerted M. de Rênal to the sorry state of his conjugal felicity. Rênal agonized ingloriously, caught between the wish to be vengefully manly and the fear of ridicule, compounded by the loss of his wife's personal fortune. Prompt countermeasures neutralized his fears, as the lovers managed to ascribe to Valenod, the poorhouse director and his rival for supremacy in Verrières, the anonymous missive, followed up swiftly by a more damaging one of their own. Complicity in perilous deception now bound Julien to Mme de Rênal by the closest ties conceivable: death and dishonor faced unflinchingly together. But prudence then dictated retreat, and Julien tasted the dubious joys of his rise in the world: lionized by the opposition, he discovered the saddest truth of all. In a reactionary regime, the bourgeois Liberal opposition differed from the ultramontane government party by the open grossness of their appetites, unveiled by upper-class manners, and by their powerless longing to join as equal partners in the official looting of the Nation's resources. This further step in his political education gave way to the hero's obligatory descent into the underworld[7] of the Besançon seminary fumingly underwritten by the much battered Rênal.

Physically, morally, spiritually the stay in the priestly stronghold at Besançon was to be a death by which the hero's resolve had to be tempered, in the bitter waters of a modern Styx. Physically, the ugliness, the total confinement, the browbeating hostility caused Julien to faint on the threshold, under the terrible gaze of Father Pirard, the least harmful of his jailers. Morally he was surrounded with spies, loathed for his failure to toady convincingly, suspected of brains and integrity (i.e. Jansenism[8]). Spiritually his shield of hypocrisy melted in the searing fires of the Big Lie: a vigilance of every moment scarcely sufficed to ward off the unblinking gaze of a thousand eyes, armed by self-interest grafted on native inclination, to see through his merely willed mendacity. Relief had to be improvised in the eleventh hour by an unlikely trio of saviors: Father Chas-Bernard, grateful for a first-rate student, called upon him to help adorn the cathedral for the feast of *Corpus Domini*. Julien's agility and courage took him forty feet above the main altar to crown the canopy with plumes. The literal uplift conferred by this brief escape upward, amid ringing of bells and heavy brocade, from the dispiriting mire of his incarceration was soon matched by promotion to an assistant tutorship, the gift of his stern master Father Pirard. With this followed a private room, the precious gift of distance from his grubby peers, without which this fierce loner might not have survived. Finally the Marquis de La Mole, the eminent and wealthy protector of Father Pirard, took him on as his secretary, as a gesture of gratitude to a faithful overseer of his interests in some long-standing local litigation, removing him from this den of thieves, upon the worthy abbé's resignation from his beleaguered post.

On the face of it, Julien's arrival in Paris in La Mole's employ must have struck him as a direct and bodily translation from hell into heaven, from the hell where he had seemed both defeated and imprisoned, to the spacious heaven of his ambition. The Hôtel de la Mole came as close to the center of power in 1830 France as he could dream to reach. Dry, faintly supercilious, admirably polite and obliging, infinitely bored, the elegant denizens of its splendid salons comported themselves as the born rulers they felt themselves to be. Julien was awed but undaunted. Though he too, like his creator, spelled *cela* with two l's on his first day at his desk, and fell from horseback on his first jaunt with the Comte Norbert, the son of the house, he did not let himself be condescended to. He laughed off the fall, reporting it at table himself, and persisted with the daily rides until he mastered the horse. His paperwork soon reflected his superior ability. Saturnine and unbending, he won the respect, and soon the affection, of the marquis, whose gout he could soothe by reading to him selectively and discriminatingly out of the day's papers. He earned promotion from the black coat of his official clerical capacity to the blue coat of trusted and amusing companionship. A light diplomatic assignment to England brought him the indispensable decoration. A duel with the foppish Chevalier de Beauvoisis, whose card had been filched by his coachman, to be hurled at Julien's face in a traffic wrangle,[9] resulted in the rumor that Julien was the natural son of the Duc de Chaulnes (Beauvoisis could scarcely brag he had fired a shot at a little scribbler employed by La Mole!)

Julien's rise, by means far more genteel and congenial than he had envisioned in his austere beginnings, had taken him to the brink of naturalization into the aristocracy, where his native refinement, his cult of the will, his thirst for greatness seemed to have marked out his berth from the beginning of time. Was this the promise of the Revolution fulfilled? Had his iron determination to lift his means within sight of his lofty goals so easily prevailed? There were uneasy twinges that belied this interpretation, for they cast a pall over the outward brilliance of his fortunes.

A secret mission took Julien to a conspiratorial meeting at which the highest lay and ecclesiastical personages of the regime seriously considered the advisability of calling in a foreign army, to quell the inevitable revolt of the youth of the nation, faced with perpetual exclusion from power. There could be little doubt in his mind which services he would eventually be called to render in the cause of the old nobility, quaking for its new-won privileges, founded on nothing more than the backlash of Waterloo. His first use of the rights of patronage bestowed on him for his faithful attendance on the gout-ridden marquis left no doubt in his own mind which way he found himself drifting. Valenod having replaced Rênal as mayor of Verrières, Julien had his father named to the poorhouse directorship thus left vacant: scarcely a forward-looking move, or an act of charity toward the poor! The sense of his betrayal did not come home to him, however, until he learned that the symbol of integrity in that same town, the mathematician Gros,[10] had been put forward by departmental deputation for the lottery bureau, which Julien had caused to be awarded, on a whim, to the toadying fool whose abject bid had caused him amusement.

By the kind of topsy-turvy logic which so often presided over Julien's fate, the doubts that gnawed at him at that time helped to move him to the pinnacle of his worldly achievement, a success which then in turn triggered the dissolution of his ideological quandary, in the apparent surrender of his worldly aims. The somber mood induced by his sense of his own betrayal flared out in silent contempt for the high-born scoundrels and their retinue of toad-eaters with whom he felt himself surrounded. The elegant fops who adorned the La Mole salons, clustering in witty insignificance around the greatest heiress in France, the proud, caustic, self-willed, beautiful Mathilde de La Mole, excited his particular resentment. The sense of his own superiority over these millionaire horse fanciers, whose hereditary bravery encompassed neither the utterance of a novel idea nor the first inkling of the kind of lonely, total war he had had to declare on society and fight all his life long, drove him to haughty silence, on his little stool on the outskirts of this brilliant circle. Mathilde, romantic soul that she was, who wore mourning on the anniversary of the execution of a sixteenth-century forebear, Boniface de La Mole, who died for the love of a lady, began to wonder about this enigmatic young man, whose pride shone with a fire unknown among the well-bred types whose courtship so mortally bored her. Catching a glimpse of his somber animation, in the company of a Spanish conspirator, Count Altamira, on whose head there was a price, she began to divine in him a kind of greatness, that of a Danton, ravening among those helpless sheep promised to the guillotine, the descendants of Boniface de La Mole. True nobility had passed into the hearts of the plebeians—like the fiery, perhaps even murderous Julien—just as the death penalty had come to be the only honor that could not be bought.

The conversation with Altamira which *crystallized*[11] Mathilde's incipient passion for Julien is perhaps Stendhal's nearest approach to a clear formulation of the ambiguities, not unlike his own, which beset his hero's political commitment. *Engagé dans quoi?* we might well ask in the first place. Julien's cause does not possess even the embryonic political relevance exhibited by Altamira's struggle to earn Spain a charter. Though he sees his will to power as clearly in the service of the oppressed, no move so far concretely embodies this larger purpose. More seriously still, since it might be argued that the time for action hadn't come, no hint is given of any thought of organization, of translating his private dream into political action. Julien's instincts as a loner seem in fact to preclude such a development. In this context of political unrealism, the conversation with Altamira takes on its full importance. What is being argued is the weightiest question of all, the searing crux of political action: must one be prepared to spill blood in a good cause? Julien's position veers wildly, from the anxious concern of the feeling man, who recoils, aghast, from the blood-thirstiness of the partisan spirit (Altamira's sister danced for joy at the death of Ney) to the airy salon activism that had so damaged Stendhal's own reputation in the eyes of the Tracy crowd ("Wait till you've killed a man in a duel," cautions Altamira sadly, as he prates of having "three men killed to save the lives of four" [306]). It is the sense of muddle—private aims brilliantly realized, general goals vaguely and not quite responsibly groped for—which in part lent to his features that virile hue of resolution with which Mathilde was falling in love. Her love in turn tipped the balance disproportionately in favor of private realization. Impetuously she gave herself, then recoiled in wounded pride, precipitating an imbroglio of mutual agonizing, each overcome in turn by longing as the other's pride forced him (or her) to back away. In the end Mathilde is made pregnant and the enraged marquis, ruffled for once into swearing like a coachman, reluctantly packs up his dream of a duchess's stool for his daughter. Julien is sent off to earn his spurs as Lieutenant Julien Sorel de la Vernaye: the red uniform of heroic ambition is his, together with full membership in the ancient feudal nobility it had been his object simultaneously to emulate and to set aside. The husband of Mathilde de La Mole had decisively humbled the pride of the gilded youth vying for the hand of the first match in France—and they numbered among them some of the most illustrious families in the Gotha, the Duc de Luz, the Marquis de Croisenois, the Comte de Caylus. As Monsieur de la Vernaye he need fear no slight his sword could not avenge. Unquestionably a pinnacle had been reached which might excusably have turned the head of the little carpenter's son from Verrières.

Julien was saved from such a fate by a bolt from the blue. Under the dictation of her new confessor, Mme de Rênal had penned an answer to the marquis's inquiries, that branded Sorel a cold-blooded seducer, whose method it was to gain control over a household by seeking "to seduce the woman who has the most influence there" [452]. Streaking through half of France in the course of a paragraph, Julien fired a pistol shot at the *ferne Geliebte,* at her who stood thereby revealed to himself and to the reader as his one true love, a shot that marked the loss forever of the coveted red coat, exchanged without a second thought for the ignominious grays of prison garb. Thwarted ambition, a lover's rage at being maligned and utterly cast aside by the only woman he had really loved, relief at the chance of resounding and decisive action in the increasing remoteness of his present circumstances from the self he really knew—all these may have weighed on that impulsive decision, as might also the wish to make a dramatic end—*finir en beauté.* Passion, in any event, had taken over from ambition—that passion, dear to Stendhal's heart, which threw calculation to the winds and lost itself in the object of its longing. To shoot Mme de Rênal, was not the most logical, sensible, *French* way of proving his love: but it was love's unreasoning *Italian* way of making itself felt. And it worked.

Much more perplexing is the plea to the jury by which Julien, in effect, browbeat that respectable assemblage, half won over to leniency by the powerful exertions of his former enemy, the Vicar-general de Frilair, into pronouncing the death sentence on him. Weariness with the prospect of owing his life to Mathilde, when all his thoughts went out to Mme de Rênal, may have played its part in his suicidal challenge to the jury's class interests. Yet the incongruousness of Julien's appealing to his peasant origins to give his condemnation the character of an act of bourgeois vengefulness, when his whole life stood witness to his successful onslaught on the middle class and his utter repudiation of all trace of peasant character in himself, demands further explanation. As he chose to drag into his trial the red herring of class warfare—calculated to rouse the antagonism he claimed to expose—this act of self-destruction must be placed in the context of political action. Julien's meteoric rise in the world, as we have seen, had been achieved at the cost of his political mission. Though he still held to his convictions, to his perhaps largely sentimental identification with the have-not class, he was to be effectual only in furthering his private interests, in removing Monsieur de la Vernaye from the class he wished to lead into the Promised Land. Lacking true political vocation—the ability to formulate a program and organize a movement—this freebooter of the betrayed Revolution could do no more than exemplify, by stealth, in his own person, a promise of individual greatness the Revolution had intended for all. The only way to reconcile success and integrity—virtue and *virtù*—was in a public proclamation of an otherwise invisible challenge, one that would cost him his life. By labeling his private campaign an episode in the general warfare of the mighty against the dispossessed, Julien managed to throw his life away in a cause he felt powerless to advance by his own success.

Hence the romantic resolution of *The Red and the Black*—the fleeting bliss of reunion with Mme de Rênal in the death cell, Mathilde burying Julien's head in the manner of the beloved of Boniface de La Mole—rests on a solid grounding of political assertion. In Restoration France, circa 1830, a peasant lad may rise to a position befitting his abilities; but it must be at the cost of the most stringent application of a policy of disciplined deception. A single moment of genuine feeling may cost him his career. Success, on the other hand, spells automatic betrayal of the interests his rise was intended to promote. Having infiltrated the ruling class, he would either merge with it, or find himself quickly excluded—and as powerless as he had been at the start. The sole challenge left open, therefore, was ringing denunciation: and it was this Julien had seized on, from the unique vantage point of the prisoner's box.

II *The Vital Center*

In *The Red and the Black* Stendhal had pitted a gifted young peasant against a regime that sought to return to power the titled remnant of a long-vanished feudal aristocracy. *Lucien Leuwen* was more daring by far: in it the writer undertook to expose the less dramatic, but no less poignant, confrontation of the gifted youth who rebels against his own class, under a regime nominally devoted to the interests of all. Refugees from "consensus politics" in the America of yesterday may find in this account of life under Louis-Philippe's[12] bourgeois monarchy the rueful pleasure of recognition. The book certainly owes to its tackling of the politics of evasion its curious position in the Stendhal canon, somewhat akin to that of *The Sentimental Education* in the writings of Flaubert. The touchstone of connoisseurship, it often leaves the casual reader cold, while among *the happy few* some perversely rank it their favorite of the three great novels, as the truest to their hero's unmistakable manner.

In any event, *Lucien Leuwen,* undertaken at Civita-Vecchia in 1835, is an unfinished novel. The blame has been placed variously on the writer's distance from the Parisian scene, the matrix of his imagination (Martineau), or on the absence of a proper mythical framework (G. Durand). I incline to see the unfinished state of the novel as emblematic of its subject: the search for personal relevance and integrity in the morass of middle-of-the-road *(juste milieu)* politics. The Restoration monarchy obliged its enemies by presenting them with the barefaced villainy of the revocation of the Constitution granted by Louis XVIII, thus plunging the country back into serfdom (or so it seemed). A peasant could declare war on such a regime, and though the flabbiness of Liberal opposition led Julien to settle his curse on both the houses of the political community, a clash of opposing wills, clearly defined by class interests, arose unmistakably, blending romance with ideology. Matters stood far otherwise under the July monarchy. Brought into power by a popular uprising, the regime consummated the displacement of the landed aristocracy by the moneyed middle class. Beyond that it would not go: in the words of its most celebrated Prime Minister, Guizot, the policy of its government was *to stand pat.* Where the reactionary Bourbons had looked elsewhere—to the past, and *ultra montes* to Rome and papal infallibility—for their dreams, the conservative Orléans monarch was content, prosily, to sustain the present, to freeze existing social arrangements by enshrining the status quo. Keeping down the working class and keeping out the old ruling class, the bourgeois king hewed to the policy of *juste milieu:* the "vital center" of a budding industrial-commercial establishment intent on peace and stability, at whatever cost. The cost turned out to be a stodgy foreign policy that quite failed to stir the minds of a youth brought up on the Napoleonic legend; and at home, a staunch refusal to enlarge the electorate or respond to the plight of the early industrial proletariat, which eventually knit the alliance of workers and libertarians that brought down the regime in the revolution of 1848.

To *do* such a setup in a novel Stendhal had the acumen to select a hero whose plight, though on the surface unheroic, had the considerable merit, novelistically, of being emblematic of the age that had shaped his quest. Lucien Leuwen, the pampered son of an amiable banker, had to earn his spurs by breaking with a world eager to smother him in the rewards of complicity, just as Julien Sorel, the son of a grasping peasant, had had to renounce the path of glory, to wrench some self-respect out of a world he could only beat into submission by deviousness. Julien had nothing, and therefore had to conceal his ambition beneath the black cassock of feigned humility. Lucien, who had everything, could only begin to earn something he could call his own by serving a state he thoroughly despised. Open rebellion merely led to expulsion from the Ecole Polytechnique, and his republican sentiments, had they become generally known, would have branded him of unsound mind. Where the carpenter's son had risked destruction, the banker's son courted exclusion (i.e. certified political impotence) by any barefaced onslaught on a society that bred heroes only inadvertently, with the express intent to starve them into submission.

The adored son of a woman of genuine refinement, whom her witty banker husband worshiped, Lucien Leuwen had been born to the heaven of Stendhal's dreams: a world of taste, opulence, wit, and pleasure *(volupté)*. Spiritual starvation, in him, arose from emotional well-being, where Julien's had sprung from deprivation:[13] no simpleminded sociology of achievement presides over the destinies of the elect. Whether it originates in the shack or the mansion, the path of heroism is equally arduous and lonely.

Lucien's first move, after earning his expulsion from the Ecole polytechnique by breaking an order confining him to quarters, on a day of student riot against the regime, was to accept a lieutenant's commission in a Lancers' regiment, wangled for him by his father's influential friends. He was launched on his course, in other words, by a powerful and solicitous parent, *for his own good.* His unassuming manner did not give him the kind of salon presence that others might feel they had to reckon with. The taint of republican leanings, moreover, had to be removed if the youth were to be rescued from the limbo of intellectual seriousness. Hence the army, which a lingering climate of heroism redeemed from the general corruption, making it an acceptable way out (though Lucien saw himself wryly confronting the ghost of Napoleon: " *'You must have been dying of hunger to engage in this profession?'–'No, General, I wanted to follow in your footsteps.' And Lucien burst out laughing . . . ." [Green Huntsman,* 13]). To be sure, garrison life in Nancy soon laid the ghost of military glory. Dull, surly, envious fellow officers; the hopeless careerism of his commander, a wartime hero; a steady diet of café billiards resulting from social exclusion in a town dominated by resentful nobles; the necessity—common to all Stendhalian heroes under like circumstances—of staring down incipient insolence with a cold watchfulness that did violence to his natural openness and his readiness to love and emulate fellow-heroes—all this soon turned his dreams to ashes. Cut off from "the people," out of touch with his social equals, coldly received by his professional companions, Lucien had no better company to fall back upon than the honest republican journalist Gauthier, whose ideological rantings did little to overcome the sense that the party of virtue was fatally wedded to the triumph of mediocrity. *Go to America and court the goodwill of any greengrocer* is the deadly alternative to injustice and inequality that flashes through the mind of every Stendhalian hero in turn, but which Lucien was least equipped, in the circumstances of his political immurement, to brush away decisively.

A fall from horseback showed him the way out of his morass. Under the windows of the perfectly beautiful Mme de Chasteller, the young second lieutenant was thrown by his recalcitrant nag on the very day of his arrival in the garrison town. The glimpse of her proud beauty, seared into his mind by her laughter at his tumble, served to make her mistress of all his thoughts. Not until he met the eloquent hunchback Dr. Du Poirier, intellectual leader of the reactionary aristocracy of Nancy, called to his bedside months later to dress a duel wound, was Lucien enabled to crash through the high walls behind which Nancy high society mocked at Orléans soldiery, and to approach his beloved. Practically sequestered by her father, M. de Pontlevé, who, fearful of a new emigration, wished to keep in hand his widowed daughter's great fortune, Mme de Chasteller lived isolated, by choice as well, from the backbiting frivolity of her little aristocratic backwater. Her beauty, her wealth, the gentle aloofness of a dreamy soul made her a target of envy. By putting up with the grotesque antics of a society they both despise, the handsome young officer—perplexed republican in this den of feudalists—and the secluded heiress—whose Bourbon loyalties are entirely a matter of heart—edged slowly closer to a decisive meeting of minds and hearts. While a romantic resolution is narrowly averted at this stage, Lucien, by the enforced contact with the old provincial nobility with whom his perfect manners, his flawless accoutrements, his determination to please (for the sake of the beloved) allow him to mingle quite effortlessly, made another giant stride in his political education. These outsiders on the Right, in spite of their absurd pretensions and criminal designs, by paying the full price of their principled retirement from political and military life, instructed him in the sacrificial character of even a wrongheaded utopia. Though they dreamed of the restoration of their most exorbitant and unfounded privileges, these young men lived in a poverty akin to that of their despised republican counterparts, having in addition buried hopes of warlike lives dearer to them than wealth or power. His sense of the sordidness of the cause he was serving aimlessly and reluctantly was heightened the more by the sole expedition for which he was called out: a march, happily concluded in a bloodless standoff, against working men in a neighboring town, accused of having *"organized"* and *"formed a protective society"!* [258]

Envy of the interloper, who seemed to have come close to running off with the fairest prize in their midst, aroused the young bucks of Nancy's gilded set to entrust their mentor, Du Poirier, with the task of disposing of him. The diabolical doctor staged the black comedy of a pretended delivery, with Leuwen posted within sight and hearing of the removal of what purported to be Mme de Chasteller's baby. Heartbroken though not entirely won over to the thought of wickedness in a mind so candid, Lucien Leuwen, without another thought to military duty, galloped back to Paris, to report to Mme Leuwen: "Mother, I am mad. Except that my honor is intact, I am the unhappiest of men. . . . I have loved, and I have been deceived." [368]

A second career opened up for Lucien Leuwen at this low point in his sentimental life: repelled by the notion of remaining an opulent nobody all his life, he accepted manfully his father's offer of a post of confidence in the Ministry of the Interior, where the wealthy banker Leuwen had his entrées and his mutually profitable deals. Sitting astride his lofty impractical views on public morality and private honor, Lucien faced up—as he thought—to the politician's first requirement (as his father put it)—to being a *scoundrel.* Drawing the line at the spilling of blood, our misplaced Galahad marched resolutely forward. The mess that awaited him did not altogether belie his father's facetious anticipations. A trusted secret agent in the War Ministry had sought to disarm a sentinel, posing as a drunken workman. This episode in the government's campaign to undermine solidarity between the military and the lower classes backfired embarrassingly: the raw recruit turned out to be a hardy mountaineer, and Kortis, the secret agent, lay dying of a gunshot wound in the stomach. The surgeon could not be bribed to finish him off with opium: how was he to be silenced, knowing himself at death's door? Lucien was willing to extricate the Minister of the Interior, on the condition that he might treat "Kortis as tenderly as his own family" *(Telegraph,* 72). A man-to-man offer to Kortis that his widow would be generously pensioned off, together with his word as an officer that no further attempt would be made on his life thereupon did the trick. A further mission to buy off a couple of elections, in the course of which Lucien had mud literally shoveled in his face by an angry mob that discovered him for a government agent completed his initiation. The necessity of wallowing in the well-earned contempt of his fellow countrymen was as bitter a pill for that spotless hero as it was intended to be instructive to the reader, in the ways of centrist politics under a constitutional monarchy. By taking every unnecessary risk to his career, maneuvering in fact as would a cavalry general who, in a desperate pass, ordered his men to fight dismounted (thus courting ridicule on top of disaster), Lucien redeemed himself in his own eyes, while losing the election to the almost saintly opposition candidate. As he put it himself: "Although the battle seemed lost, I engaged my regiment!" [239]. He had, in fact, negotiated with the legitimist opposition, offering on his own authority 100,000 francs in gold to effect an alliance against the moderate republican candidate. The minister wired the money, but the election foundered on the rage of the waspish, ineffectual prefect who, finding himself bypassed by a 26-year-old on mission from Paris, withheld his electors from the coalition.

Upon his return to Paris Lucien discovered that his rashness, once more, had been compensated for by the latest hobby indulged in by the ebullient Leuwen senior. To the joys of private persiflage at the bumbling machinations of the scoundrels in power, in the select gathering of his wife's salon, the banker had chosen to add the headier pleasures of a public forum: he had successfully run for deputy of the Aveyron department. Public life henceforth was to be subjected to scrutiny and mercilessly scourged on yet another level, in the novel: the highest in fact, since deputy Leuwen, by his dangerous wit and assiduous courtship of a few handfuls of deputies from the "sticks," whom he molded into a bloc, wielded enough power to bring the king himself, that "electoral calculating machine," before the reader!

Leuwen *père* had required of his son, upon his return to Paris, assiduous amorous attendance on Mme Grandet, a ranking beauty with political ambitions, to scotch all rumors that he had Saint-Simonian (socialist) leanings. His mother's overwhelming fear that Lucien's disappointed love might turn his thoughts to suicide prompted the banker father to ring him round in this fashion with obligations day and night. The father's playful politics eventually merged with the son's dutiful courtship in a climax of many-pronged satire: the coldly virtuous Mme Grandet gave herself to Lucien, in exchange for ministerial promotion contrived for her fatuous incompetent husband by Leuwen *père's* influence "on high." This piece of wizardry, which resulted in the embarrassment of her falling in love with her utterly indifferent suitor (punishing them both for trifling with Eros), was to be the impenitent banker-politician's last: sudden death at this point removed him from the scene.

Delivered by financial ruin (a profitable bankruptcy suggested by his late father's chief accountant had been ruled out of the question by Lucien Leuwen, needless to say!) from the burden of power and success in a world so utterly and openly for sale, Lucien, at the end of the second part of the book, sailed for Italy as Second Secretary to the Embassy at Capel, about to embark on a third career in a third part that was never written, which presumably would have reunited him with Mme de Chasteller in the enchanting setting of a land that deserved to be called a *paysage de l'âme* for them both.

Politics under Louis-Philippe, it may be concluded, had turned into a maze without even the perverse connection with reality provided by the

Restorations's dream of a new Middle Ages. The Army held the workers at bay, turning its back on the fields of glory. The Government maneuvered shamelessly to keep itself in power, with no nobler end in view than eating its share of the budget. The nobility sulked, the people glowered, the nation—in Guizot's own words (some few years later)—was bored. The impotence of Lucien Leuwen, a hero balked in his mission—that of redeeming himself by great works from the curse of idle opulence—reflected on the personal plane the politics of the halfway house: neither forward- nor backward-looking, neither republic nor authentic monarchy, neither slave nor free. Mme de Chasteller remained inaccessible (through the fraudulence of the power-mad hunchback): the hero failed in his liberating quest of the ideal, in an age that afforded him no saving distance from the quagmire realities of fear and greed. Only the flight away from France, disburdened of power and wealth, to the Italy which harbored Stendhal himself under the immunity of modest diplomatic functions, could disengage the hero sufficiently from the ambient corruption to let love mend his plight, inviting him to soar to the heaven of his native destination.

III *Waterloo to Versailles*

Balzac's "rave" review of the comparatively unknown Stendhal's *Charterhouse of Parma* is one of the few heart-warming episodes in that chapter of literary history in which writer meets writer as live fellow genius. His one stricture against the opening chapter on the French invasion of Milan (which he would have turned into a flashback from the vantage point of Waterloo) points just as impressively to the fact that even a well-intentioned giant is not altogether to be trusted with the appreciation of another's master work; that his own genius, in fact, may blind him to what is most felicitous and original in the production of another, more subtle genius. For what Balzac missed in that exhilarating irruption of Napoleon's ragged citizen army upon this soil which had seen ancient liberties crushed, a gifted people infantilized by oppression, all spirit smothered in ennui, was the unique confrontation of the stupid, servile, doddering Past with the vibrant, joyous, liberating Present that was the quintessence of Stendhal's Enlightenment joke on modern politics. Lieutenant Robert, putative father of the novel's hero Fabrizio, artfully disguising the strings that tied his soles to his shoes with blacking, to make a decent appearance before the Marchesa del Dongo, in whose palace he was billeted (the Marchese having prudently fled, leaving his beautiful young wife to the tender mercies of the French ogres), stands in unforgettable contrast to that other memorable figure, the Marchese himself, decoding his Austrian Emperor's messages in the full regalia of a court chamberlain: Youth smiling winningly in tatters, Age grimly foolish in its silks and diamonds!

France and Italy also find themselves at last happily united under the pen of one whose love for Milan has seemed to eclipse what he owed to the land of his birth. The France of Rousseau and of the Revolution, the France that had given birth to the modern and broken with the gilded slavery of the ancient was alone worthy, in the charming person of Lieutenant Robert, to be united in true matrimony with the spirit of Italy, the abandoned Marchesa, whose lord and master, when he could safely return from the border fortress where he cowered, would assume unloving paternity of the hero, born (as far as he was to know) from his own cold embraces. In Fabrizio the mythical union of the high and the low, of ruler and nation, of popular and noble blood, was to be consummated literally, as it had been only figuratively in the rise of Julien Sorel de la Vernaye, bastard presumptive of the Duc de Chaulnes.

Fabrizio it was then—the last-born, the beloved Benjamin of Stendhal's imagination—who would in person accomplish the pilgrimage to Waterloo: not fictitiously, or in yearning retrospect, but, miraculously, *in the present* and at the age of sixteen. The wanderings of a paladin fresh from the reading of Tasso and the storied genealogy of the del Dongos through a battlefield racked by gunfire, under the expert guidance of a sturdy female army provisioner, were to form the nearest sequel to *Don Quixote* the nineteenth century was to know. Fabrizio lifted from horseback when the general's mount is shot from under him; Fabrizio anxiously deliberating whether he had been at a battle, and whether that battle *was* Waterloo; Fabrizio wounded, not by enemy fire, but by French deserters he sought to keep from running off, had drained in one day the cup of illusion. War was neither heroic nor ennobling; women were not won by his sword, but mostly mothered or nursed him out of trouble; a great event in history did not wear the look of a great event in the eye of the participants. Napoleon at Waterloo buried the hopes of the Revolution for France and for all Europe, not as a titan at bay, but as the no longer competent military dictator of a demoralized nation. Journeying back to Milan under the passport of a barometer salesman, Fabrizio was soon acquainted with the melancholy face of day-to-day police state reality. Denounced to the Austrian authorities by his elder brother Ascanio, Fabrizio discovered that a lifelong exile from the sites of his childhood was to be the price exacted for the first (and last) political act in which, not much more than a child, he had engaged—inspired by an eagle's flight.

At this point Conte Mosca enters upon the scene—that unique projection of the author in late middle age (i.e. at the time of writing)—to watch over the idealized version of his younger self, the most unreconstructed of Stendhal's political innocents. Conte Mosca, unillusioned idealist that he was, after serving with distinction in Napoleon's Spanish campaigns,[14] had ended up as Prime Minister in a despotic Parma, minimizing bloodshed by humoring a moderately tyrannical sovereign, to whom he managed to make himself indispensable by taking upon himself the ridicule of his master's fears (looking literally and imperturbably—in fact he insisted on looking—for skulking Liberals under palace beds in the dead of night!) This worldly, witty, humane politician perpetrated the ultimate joke of figuring as the *ultra*[15] on the chessboard of Parmesan politics, the official Liberal opposition being made up of a pack of scoundrels and murderous dunderheads headed, respectively, by Marchesa Raversi and General Fabio Conti. Mosca fell in love with Fabrizio's aunt, Gina Pietranera, the beautiful, headstrong, brilliant widow of a Piedmontese general in the service of France, left penniless by her husband's early death in a rigged duel. The Conte had little fortune (for he was as honest as he was clear-sighted) and he felt the ridicule of his position, as the power behind a minuscule throne: his lucidity served him as handsomely as his passion, with a woman who had learned the ways of the world in the highest and the lowest fortune, and who was Stendhalian enough to smile on passionate lucidity, as she had laughed at moneyed fools.

The Duchessa Sanseverina (a marriage of convenience with the aged Duke, off to ambassadorial glory, had provided Gina with a palazzo and a station in life) cut a brilliant figure at the court of Parma, playfully advancing the Conte's interests while baffling his foes, by providing the ruling Ernesto-Ranuce IV with the only salon where he could not be bored. That prince, though the realities of nineteenth-century politics led him to fear for his life, preferred to think of himself as a latter-day Louis XIV, his court a Versailles. The exiguousness of the kingdom, on the other hand, placed him at the galling mercy of the independent-minded Duchessa, who could at any time pack off (as she once had cause to threaten to do) and make this small-town despot the laughter of all Naples. Fabrizio was to provide the occasion of salving the ruler's wounded vanity with an application of ferociousness and perfidy calculated to make him feel that he was king indeed.

For Fabrizio had not ceased to be dearer to his youthful, infatuated aunt (though she knew it not) than life itself. The Conte's advice had turned the young exile into a seminarian: the prelacy seemed the only fitting niche for a gifted aristocrat, the only stronghold where his gifts could not harm him, his noble blood not stand in his way. We have come full circle from Julien's heroic choice: a man of character must hide his strength, whatever the class he is born into! On his arrival in Parma, fresh from his clerical training in Naples, the young del Dongo made a poor impression on the sovereign: his heartfelt absolutist doctrines (for he had the true aristocrat's indifference to ideas, and therefore blithely espoused what he had been taught) in a man of his obvious superiority seemed careless parody. But the Church stood by him: the plebeian-born Archbishop Landriani was greatly moved at counting a del Dongo among his clerical retinue.

Having discovered, before it dawned on her, his beloved aunt's infatuation with himself, which he despaired of returning, Fabrizio sought diversion in various love affairs, one of which led him into a brawl with a jealous mountebank he was forced to kill in self-defense. Ernesto-Ranuce IV saw his chance: trumped-up charges, doctored testimony, a special court of justice packed by the infamous Rassi, his unscrupulous minister of justice, resulted in a sentence of twenty years' detention in the Parma fortress. The Duchessa's handwriting forged at Marchesa Raversi's instructions baited a trap which landed Fabrizio, then safely in hiding, into solitary confinement at the top of the redoubtable Farnese tower.

"It is a ridiculous thing, a court, . . . but it is amusing" (Anchor, 110) Contessa Pietranera had earlier confided to Fabrizio's mother. The ferocious puerility of Louis XIV politics in the age of liberal aspirations and the daily press, all of which are made to serve the private vanities of men in power, offered in the fate of the guileless, handsome, gifted, spirited Fabrizio a sobering corrective to that light-hearted view. The battle of wits by which Conte Mosca, sensible and feeling, kept the sanguinary crew of Rassi and consorts from binding the sovereign to their will by ties of spilled blood, though he engaged in it laughingly, was played out on the brink of human disaster. Sense, courage, dignity, love of homeland were the crimes that rated torture and death; terror was the mainstay of power; caprice, the utmost perfection of its exercise. Laughable and murderous, the court of an absolute sovereign who ruled over a dot on the map thus caught up in unforgettable miniature all the iniquity, all the absurdity, all the frivolity which the politics of reaction, in a grander setting, could manage to render plausible. Fabrizio in his tower, blissfully all-absorbed in the love of Clelia Conti, the daughter of his vengeful jailer, while far, far below the Duchessa maneuvered desperately to insure his escape (the last thing on his mind), highlighted, on the vertical scale this time, that same distance between the ridiculous and the sublime: the politics of repression viewed from the angelic height of reciprocated love.

Fabrizio did escape: talk of poison drove Clelia to take a hand in Gina's elaborate plans. Guards were drugged, ropes smuggled in by the hundred-yards, a fabulous leap successfully taken. The Duchessa fled, illuminating her castle at Sacca while Parma was flooded by her orders. Ernesto-Ranuce IV, whose persecution of Fabrizio had been a blow aimed solely at herself, died a suspicious death advertised as a hunting accident. The outlaw Ferrante Palla, poet and revolutionary, had struck that blow for the love of the divine Sanseverina. Mosca, who had been kept in the dark, held the mob at bay and saved the throne for the Crown Prince, whom he proceeded to serve, as head, this time, of the Liberal party. The well-intentioned youth proved a pricklier, less sensible sovereign than his vain but at bottom quite professional statesman of a father. The Duchessa returned, and the royal youth soon pined for her charms, while the Sanseverina palace shared with the salon of the Queen Mother (whose tenuous hold on her son the Duchessa endeavored to strengthen) the privilege of unalloyed gaiety. To secure Fabrizio's exoneration became the end of all policy for the Duchessa, together with the promotion of the Marchese Crescenzi, whose offer of betrothal Clelia Conti had accepted, to atone for her share in Fabrizio's escape and her father's discomfiture. Gina in turn applied herself to promote a union whose very possibility was a stab at Fabrizio's unfaithful heart.

The climax of these machinations came as Fabrizio, eagerly resuming his blessed cell within sight of Clelia's aviary, awaited news of his official rehabilitation. The enraged Fabio Conti, who felt personally dishonored by his prisoner's escape, which was about to be topped off by a triumphant return to favor and power, arranged to have him poisoned. The alerted Duchessa pressed the King to dispatch a personal emissary, a concession she wrung at the price of a promise to surrender to his lust. Clelia meanwhile broke into Fabrizio's cell, and believing him at death's door gave herself to him minutes before the emissary's arrival. Fabrizio had not eaten, and survived. The Duchessa paid the exacted price and retired to Naples as Contessa Mosca della Rovere. Clelia married Crescenzi, and faithful to a vow made to the Madonna, never looked upon the face of the new archbishop of Parma, Fabrizio del Dongo, though she gave herself to him in darkness.

The logic of divine right monarchy thus flowered into the unthinkable contradictions which partake of its essence: a sovereign the more iniquitous for his being high-minded, justice secured by prostitution, an archbishop in love, a prime minister cuckolded and content. Vicious conclusions flow from silly premises. But the mixture of evil and folly which is Parma is held firmly in the perspective ordained by its size. The opening chapters had revealed the tidal wave engulfing all of Europe, lifting for a season the millstone of absolutist rule and foreign oppression that weighed down the spirit of Milan. The explosion of popular joy, the surging of elemental energies, the uplift of a nation's spirit had made clear forever what the future held in store, once the liberal creed unleashed by the Revolution had submerged the remnants of a hated past, hanging on for dear borrowed life. Parma, that droplet of undiluted absolutism in a sea of change, immortalized the hateful, laughable predicament of that past in all its justly diminished glory.

And yet, Stendhal seems to say, and yet there is more to be said about this blood-streaked grand opera regime than merely that it must be swept aside, to make room for the Republic of Virtue. The republic is austere; it is just, but dull. While Mosca weighed the qualifications of every judge to sit on Fabrizio's review board, Stendhal commented tellingly:

From the whole business one can derive this moral, that the man who mingles with a court compromises his happiness, if he is happy, and, in any event, makes his future depend on the intrigues of a chambermaid. On the other hand in America, in the Republic, one has to spend the whole weary day paying serious court to the shopkeepers in the street, and must become as stupid as they are; and there, one has no Opera. [444]

Life in Parma was beset with perils none the less real for being the work of buffoons, but the game of disarming their traps and hoisting the foe on his own petard was heady prescription for *ennui,* and characters of the quality of Mosca and the Duchessa clearly thrived on it. To become an archbishop in order to survive as a man of mettle in a booby-trapped court is a strange necessity for a Romantic hero: but the ability to view it as just such a necessity, and no more, affords Fabrizio unparalleled freedom—while it secures Stendhal's little joke at the solemnities of Church practice. Where else but in this insane Parma could a man enjoy the bliss of earthly passion together with the deserved reputation of spotless faith and unrelenting charity? Where else could the same Prime Minister exercise the same beneficent authority as the nominal head, successively, of the Liberal and the *ultra* parties?

Stendhal's fundamental ambivalence regarding the happiness of the greater number, which in his eyes summed up the doctrine of freedom and justice proclaimed by the Revolution, is embodied most tellingly in his heroes. Julien mounts the scaffold to escape the contradiction inherent in his rise to personal power: the happiness of the many necessarily recedes before the advance of their self-appointed champion, soon to be engulfed by the interests he has managed to infiltrate. Lucien is disarmed by a regime that cloaks its contradictions in a pretended concern for the welfare of all: neither military nor political action makes sense in the morass of electoral manipulation. Deprived of the chance of a meaningful fight, he abandons himself without remorse to the lure of private happiness, to the longed-for union with purity and high-mindedness in the person of Mme de Chasteller. Fabrizio marks the high and the low point on this scale of political dedication and effectiveness. As a volunteer for Waterloo, as a del Dongo on the archiepiscopal throne of Parma, he disposes of resources of direct participation in the events of his time denied by birth *and* time to the other two. But Waterloo was an exercise in futility, and power eludes the man of birth and accomplishments in a court solely preoccupied with vanity and caprice. As Fabrizio discovered in his meditation on the banks of Lake Como, his position—the basis for any possible effectiveness—rested ultimately on *privilege:*

"After all," he said to himself at length, with the lustreless eye of a man who is dissatisfied with himself, "since my birth gives me the right to profit by these abuses, it would be a signal piece of folly on my part not to take my share, but I must never let myself denounce them in public." This reasoning was by no means unsound; but Fabrizio had fallen a long way from that elevation of sublime happiness to which he had found himself transported an hour earlier. The thought of privilege had withered that plant, always so delicate, which we name happiness. [163]

The dilemma is unbroken and quite certainly insoluble. The hero's finer feelings, which mark him out as a hero in an age that no longer gives scope to personal endeavor, balk at a fulfillment purchased at the cost of others' misery. Yet the justice for which he would strive promises to erase him and all finer feelings from the face of the earth. Shopkeeper morality has no room for magnanimity. Hence a flight into the higher sphere of a love hedged with impossibilities: the Madonna-bound Marchesa Crescenzi, whose perilous vow ultimately plunges him into the open grave of the Charterhouse. Politics, in sum, while it forms the hero's highest aspirations, cannot at the same time require the duty of self-annihilation without more ado. Another land, *terra incognita,* heaves into sight to claim his allegiance, for the preservation of that in himself (or in any self) which alone is worth preserving.

CHAPTER 2

Terra Incognita

I have no wish to be understood by
anyone not born for music: would that I
could write in a sacred tongue.
Promenades dans Rome

PERHAPS the most endearing trait of the Stendhalian hero is that he
stumbles into his inheritance of love, for which he alone believes
himself unfit. Eros is a god who prefers to compel reverence: his votaries
are often recruited among those who had not before even heard of his
name. So strong is Stendhal's sense that inexperience is the first
requirement of that divine seizure[1] that in his first novel, *Armance,* the
hero's romantic quandary is founded on *physical* incapacity. That he went
to such lengths does not give us leave to read the subsequent novels (oh
Freudians!) as exercises in impotence *manquée!* Rather, it points to the
fact that the heart must not be confused with the flesh, any more than
with the mind. Love is the terra incognita that beckons to the hero from
birth, as the lost homeland where he will find that his dreams were not
merely dreams, but in a way memories, and quite certainly anticipations.
To fall wholly in love is given only to the elect, *the happy few:* for the
miracle of finding another soul of the same stamp in a world inhabited by
mechanical dolls and evil-minded buffoons is sufficient to raise the whole
gruesome comedy of existence to the level of sheer poetry (as it had for
Stendhal in the discovery of Tasso and Shakespeare). Hence the romance
of each of the great novels is essentially the itinerary from ignorance or
unbelief of a lover who took himself for someone utterly foreign to love: a
conversion, in brief.

I *Peasant to Paladin*

Two things stood in the way of self-discovery in love for Julien Sorel:
what he was, and what he dreamed of being. To take the latter first,
dreams and the bookishness that feeds on dreams were the stuff that set

him apart, and the paradoxical means of his rise in the "real" world. The New Testament in Latin took him successfully through the first fiery hoop of his social ascension: overawed and disarmed, the Verrières establishment had to make room for a feat of memory that so perfectly summed up, in its pointless complication, their own sense of the higher culture. The further marvel of it was, of course, that scripture and De Maistre[2] were merely a looking glass in which the ruling class was invited to find reflected the beliefs it wished on the lower orders. Behind that protective screen Julien dreamed his own dreams, inscribed in Rousseau's *Confessions* and the victory bulletins of the Grand Army, and concentrated in that portrait of Napoleon he concealed beneath his mattress (and bade the agitated Mme de Rênal remove to safety, without a glance at its features). The dreams induced in the little boy by the heroic tales of the surgeon-major, later to be driven underground by the triumph of the clergy (as Stendhal would have us view the Restoration), mapped out the life plan of the carpenter's son as he determined to step on the stage of history. His very ambition, in other words, marked him out as a dreamer. Later on, in the seminary, when his bold plan to outface an age of hypocrisy with hypocrisy double-dyed foundered on the shoals of a reality uglier and blacker than he could have merely *dreamed,* the ineffectual side of a dreamer's nature was to come to the fore. The death's-head pallor of the porter's face, the ferocious ugliness of Father Pirard, barking at him in a setting of unparalleled sordidness, sent him into a dead faint. And during his brief release, at Father Chas's urging, to help adorn the cathedral, the ringing of the bells induced a reverie that led the author to comment:

> He will never make a good priest, nor a good administrator. Natures yielding to emotion like this are good at most to make artists only.
>
> Here Julien's presumption bursts into the full light of day. Some fifty, maybe, of his fellow seminarists, made attentive to the real things in life on learning of the universal hatred of priests and the Jacobinism lurking in ambush behind every hedge, would have thought, on hearing the great bell of the cathedral, of nothing but the bell-ringer's wages. They would have studied, with all the mathematical accuracy of Barème, the question of whether the degree of emotion felt by the public was worth the money these bell-ringers were paid. Had Julien wished to consider the material interests of the cathedral, his imagination, overstepping the mark, would have thought of how to save forty francs on the upkeep of the building, and let slip the chance of avoiding the outlay of twenty-five centimes. (207)

A man of dreams, like the Joseph of Thomas Mann's reflections, Julien trod unknowing the path of true love: but the very nature of his dream, his fancied politico-heroic vocation, blinded him to this truth in the very act of signaling it to another. For Mme de Rênal was fatally attracted to a being as different from (and essentially indifferent to) his surroundings as she was herself. A gentle, retiring, dreamy woman, she harked gratefully back to the quiet solitude of convent school in the midst of the loud, bustling, wealth-intoxicated masculine world into which she had been thrown—her sole refuge the care of her children. She was to be moved as much by Julien's somber pride, the sense of brooding on loftier, secretive matters which he exuded, as she was relieved by his soft, childlike appearance and his gentle treatment of his little charges. But here there came into play the first-mentioned obstacle to their love: *what he was*.

The first meeting of Julien Sorel and Mme de Rênal had something of the miraculous quality with which Rousseau, in a celebrated page of his *Confessions,* endowed his first encounter, on a Palm Sunday, with Mme de Warens:

Madame de Rênal was coming out of the French window leading from the drawing-room into the garden, with the graceful ease and liveliness natural to her when no man's eyes were on her, when, just by the front door, she noticed a young peasant, still almost a child, whose face was extremely pale and bore the mark of recent tears. He was wearing a spotlessly white shirt and carried under his arm a very clean and tidy jacket of purple rateen.

This young peasant had such a fair complexion and his eyes were so gentle that Madame de Rênal's somewhat romantic nature made her at first imagine it might be some young woman in disguise who had come to ask a favor of the Mayor. She pitied the poor young thing, standing unable to move in front of the door, and evidently not daring to lift a hand to pull the bell. Madame de Rênal went up to him, her mind for the moment distracted from the bitter grief the tutor's arrival caused her. Julien, whose face was turned towards the door, did not see her approaching. He was startled when a gentle voice said close to his ear: "What brings you here, my boy?"

Julien turned round sharply and, struck by the very gracious look on Madame de Rênal's face, partly forgot his shyness. Very soon, astonished by her beauty, he forgot everything, even why he had come. Madame de Rênal had to repeat her question.

"I've come here as tutor, madam," he said to her at last, utterly ashamed of the tears he was doing his best to wipe away.

Madame de Rênal was left speechless. They stood very close together, looking at each other. Julien had never met anyone so well-dressed, especially a woman with such a dazzlingly beautiful complexion, who had spoken to him so gently. Madame de Rênal gazed at the large, round teardrops, halted in their passage down this young peasant's cheeks, which had been at first so pale and were now so pink. Very soon she began to laugh, with all a girl's irresponsible gaiety. She was laughing at herself, finding it impossible to comprehend the full extent of her happiness. What! was that the tutor she had pictured to herself as a shabby, slovenly priest, who would come to scold and beat her children!

"What, sir," she said at last, "so you know Latin?"

The term "sir" astonished Julien so much that he paused to reflect a moment.

"Yes, madam," he said shyly.

Madame de Rênal was so happy that she ventured to say to Julien: "You won't scold these poor children too much, will you?"

"I scold them!" said Julien in amazement. "And why?" (46-47)

The amazed relief, the delight of each to find the other gentle, attractive and outside the run of common experience (a beautiful, kind-spoken employer, a tidy, pink-cheeked Latinist—both of them shy!) was certainly more than sufficient to plant in them both the seed of love that time would crystallize.[3] But Julien's embattled stance, his sense of his own difference from that fine lady who surely must be laughing up her sleeve at the shabby little peasant tutor, was soon to poison those pure waters. Class consciousness, converted into class warfare by the cry "To arms!" which ruled his dream self, intervened between his dazed perception of Mme de Rênal's unaffected charm and the stern resolution to do or die which he derived therefrom. Tender feelings vanished in the drawing up of an order of battle. Madame de Rênal was to fall, as the first installment in a program of conquest. Pleasure fled, duty resumed its iron grip on a heart attuned to the victories at Austerlitz and Wagram. The hand whose fleeting touch against his own had thrilled him in the dark must be seized and held, at an immense risk to himself—to them both, in fact. Mme de Rênal's own innocence, her sublime ignorance of what the dreariest novel-reading chit could have recognized in an instant as her incipient infatuation with the high-minded, eloquent, and good-looking Latin tutor served to complicate further Love's game of blind man's buff. Neither knew enough to foresee where the game would lead: secure in her misapprehension of her own feelings, Mme de Rênal hushed up her misgivings, while Julien, hypnotized by a strategy of conquest, spurred himself on to he knew not what victory. Having impulsively sworn to himself to honor a promise to appear in her room at two in the morning, that fatal hour struck for him as had the third cock-crow for Saint Peter. Unlike the saint, he would not deny the god of his own will. Scarcely alive from the violence he did himself to obey the summons of his self-ap-pointed duty, Julien collapsed in tears in Mme de Rênal's lap, to reap the last reward of his Spartan determination—for of love there had as yet not been any question.[4]

The idyll that ensued in the enchanting setting of Vergy—brief, intense, sublimely forgetful of snares and perils—boldly crashed the gates of Paradise at the very outset of the novel. The cup of all delight was filled to the brim for him who did not even know he thirsted: taste, beauty, even voluptuousness poured into that heart both parched and immature, raising him up to manhood from depths of childish ignorance, and also churlish mistrust. The spice of danger, the thrill of secrecy, the ennobling sacrifice of religious scruple gave love an edge of mystery and pain which rendered it achingly sublime. Surrounded by loving children, stalked by hidden foes, snatching forbidden joys under the eyes of a jealous God while calmly despoiling an unsuspecting master, the lovers floated beyond good and evil, beyond risk and calculation, beyond prudence and ambition in the airy realm of pure selflessness engendered by reciprocated passion. Not even the mortal threat raised by the possible disclosure of their affair to Rênal could abate their recklessness. Skillful manipulation of that clod, armed by law with the power to destroy her utterly, earned Mme de Rênal the admiration as well as the gratitude of her lover: the test of *virtú* passed with flying colors conferred upon them that equality in daring which washed their love of all stain of treachery or self-indulgence. Julien could leave now for the frozen waters of Cocytus, to meet in the Besançon seminary the ultimate test of *his* resolution: love had earned the right to self-forgetfulness; it could, in fact, without ridicule, send him scaling the chateau walls in the dead of night, to reconquer, on his way to Paris, his mistress vainly repentant. Neither her fear of God nor yet his own manly ambition would ever prevail against a love unreflectively sublime.

Paris was to bring its own adventure, even less consciously sought after, and to all appearances symmetrical. Julien once again stumbled into bliss, once again united with a young woman scarcely less untried than himself in the mysteries of the heart. The tall, stately, blonde Mathilde de La Mole, the much sought-after daughter of the high and mighty marquis, his protector, had at first repelled Julien, on his guard once more against any possible class condescension. A vague dissatisfaction gnawed at the heart of this brilliant and somewhat bookish beauty, whose craving for the unusual, the unpremeditated, went unassuaged amid the impeccable conformists who formed her little court. That she wore mourning on the anniversary of the decapitation of her sixteenth-century forebear, Boniface de La Mole, executed under the eyes of a lady who piously preserved his head, revealed a surprising affinity, in this scion of the feudal aristocracy, with the Napoleonic mystique of the carpenter's son. Both were creatures of their dreams, each worshiped an emanation of a past directly related to his (or her) own class, each sought refuge in heroic exaltation from a toneless or an oppressive present. This affinity did not mollify Julien, but it moved Mathilde to seek a rapprochement with the proud, reserved, secretly exalted commoner, in whom she pictured a new Danton: the plebeian analogue, in other words, to the vanished grandeur of her own class. He had little thought of dancing at the ball to which she had procured him an invitation: he sought out instead the exhilarating company of Count Altamira, the proscribed Spanish conspirator. The contrast of a dedication that earned one the right to a sentence of death ("It's the only thing," thought Mathilde, "that can't be bought.") with the frivolity of her own surroundings gave Julien a decisive advantage.

This time the summons to arms came from another quarter: Mathilde herself bade Julien scale the wall to her bedroom at one o'clock in the morning. *To arms* indeed, since the youth, fearing a plot to ridicule and destroy him, came provided with pistols bulging from all pockets, with which to dispatch a few of the high-born suitors he expected to find lurking in dark corners. For Julien had reacted first with pride, then with fear, to his incalculable good fortune. To be sent for on a love tryst in her bedroom by the noblest heiress in France, who was remarkably beautiful, had been too much for the iron composure of Julien Sorel. He held in his hand the proof of his victory over the pride of suitors whose brilliant attire, whose fine horses and exalted lineage had so cruelly mortified the heart of this black-suited commoner. His second movement was no more respectable than the first: he lived in enemy land, after all; had not Mathilde, together with her fine band of mustachioed admirers, decided to cool the ardor of a little upstart, to make an end of him in a burst of contemptuous laughter, for daring to aspire so far above his station, for presuming to find in Mlle de La Mole an interest in his lowly person? Hence the dispatch of the original of her letter, inside a Bible, to the faithful Fouqué, hence the sealed instructions for publicizing the circumstances of his "accidental" death, and that quantity of pistols which was to make such a welcome conversation piece in the excruciating night these two overly imaginative but quite uninflamed lovers were to spend together perforce.

Mathilde's *amour de tête* left her as drearily unprovided for the exigencies of love—or even mere physical intimacy—as had Julien's quite irrelevant preoccupations. It was another case of backing up into terra incognita, but with this difference: that love was to remain for each of them, as they came to it in turn, a complication of pride rather than the dissolution of all pride in the bliss of self-forgetfulness. Over-reacting to the humiliation of having given herself to Julien, Mathilde first enveloped her hapless lover in a blast of icy contempt. Made vulnerable by his brief accession to felicity, Julien in his turn fell to mooning over a capricious mistress—an unwonted subservience on his part which merely increased her aloofness along with her self-hate. The pangs of a love born of rejection cannot easily be stilled, but they can be managed. Stendhal's lifelong trust in the recipes garnered from the experience of Romain Gagnon and Martial Daru could find scope in the resolution of this adventure. Julien was merely smitten: his defense then, since this was war, lay in smiting his proud captor in return. He left town on a secret mission (travel had ever been Stendhal's own first remedy, infallibly unsuccessful). In Strasbourg he culled from the lips of Prince Korasoff (overjoyed to have occasion to teach a Frenchman his trade) the secret for melting a woman's indifference: to court openly a virtuous and attractive woman of her entourage. The invaluable Korasoff in fact provided a packet of letters ready-made with which a celebrated fop had laid siege to the virtue of the most beautiful Quakeress in England. Julien dutifully copied them down, sending them one by one to that unassailable prude, the commoner-born (hence perforce irreproachable) Maréchale de Fervaques. Mathilde indeed soon wilted, and finally broke down, as the pious lady herself fairly warmed to this forbidden game.

The comedy of false courtship (Julien literally fell asleep over the blown-up theological disquisitions, addressed to the Quakeress in Richmond, with which he was to regale his jesuitical mistress) victimized—as it invariably does in Stendhal's novels—a woman given over to a masculine preoccupation with appearance and status. At one and the same time overbearing and insecure, the Maréchale was fair game: a parody of love was all that was called for to mobilize her vanity and titillate her virtue. That such a parody should yield the result of winning over Mathilde for good told much about the quality of the love that bound those two, the aspiring commoner and the headstrong aristocrat. Though Julien's enamored heart bled, as he forced himself through his paces in the cat-and-mouse game he had to play with the heart of his mistress, his nerve did not fail him: the effort clearly did not prove beyond his strength. Mathilde in the end fell limp into the arms of her Petrucchio, grateful for a taming that had taught them both anew the primacy of the will. Yet it was dependence on the will that flawed their love most decisively, as was shown by the peal of thunder in an unsuspecting sky by which Mme de Rênal signaled her reappearance into the life of an erstwhile lover.

Mathilde, who was with child, has signified to the marquis, her father, her intention of bearing Julien's offspring (and his name). The Marquis de La Mole, whose dream it had been to see his daughter a duchess, stormed and raved in vain, discomposed for the first time in his life into abuse and loud profanity. Julien weathered the squall, and Mathilde held firm. A commission in the Hussars for M. le Chevalier Julien Sorel de la Vernaye, who was to be quartered in Strasbourg, was the first step in the marquis's reluctant capitulation. A letter of inquiry to Julien's first employer then brought about Mme de Rênal's denunciation, which pictured the proud Julien as a base intriguer, who made his way in the world by seducing the woman who held greatest influence in whatever household took him in.

From a practical standpoint it may be argued that the dash across France to pump a bullet into Mme de Rênal's shoulder was perhaps the only proof Julien could give Mathilde that the letter defamed him. Yet the act itself, taken together with Julien's insistence on paying for his crime with his life (even though the wound had not been mortal), if we read it in the light of the stern letter by which he enjoined Mathilde to abandon him and never speak his name to his *son*,[5] showed him entirely wrapped up in his earlier, his only love. Revenge in this case was but the other side of the supreme importance attached to the beloved's good opinion of him. She could hate him for jilting her for another, but to be coldly despised by her was unbearable. That Julien did not act from dismay at the collapse of his worldly position is borne out by the detachment with which he was to view Mathilde's frantic maneuvers to save his head. By firing those two shots at his former mistress he had repudiated the whole airy edifice of his Parisian career. A code of honor born of love alone could justify his gesture: death to the faithless one, death to the carpenter's son betrayed in love, who now sought nothing more exalted than a lover's grave.

Julien successfully defeated Mathilde's elaborate gamble to save his life: his old enemy the Vicar-General de Frilair, won over by a bishopric through Mme de Fervaques's high ecclesiastical connections labored in vain to pack, and then seduce, the jury. The prisoner's fiery denunciation of a middle class bent on keeping himself and his fellows in their place proved stronger medicine than bribery or fear. The death sentence pronounced at his own urging had its effect: released from all wordly concerns, trampling underfoot religion and propriety Mme de Rênal fell into his arms. The world had lost its hold on two beings whose freedom lay in renouncing it. Julien's cheerful sacrifice of position, and of life itself, had taught the beloved that the shot had been fired in love: there remained nothing for it but to join him beyond mortality in an embrace that gave ultimate release. The convict and the fallen woman meeting in the death cell did not embrace in defiance of the world: they had sloughed it off altogether. Julien would mount the scaffold with little concern for honor or reputation, though he wished to make an end neither abject nor defiant: "Never had that head such poetic beauty as at the moment when it was about to fall. The sweetest moments he had known in the past in the woods of Vergy came thronging back into his mind with the most eager insistence" (508). Mme de Rênal soon joined him in the grave. It was left for Mathilde de La Mole to bury her lover's head in his favorite mountain cave, as the officiant of a cult of love consummated with another.

II *Love of a Faraway Land . . . (From a Provençal Lyric)*

The tender solicitude of a mother he loved and admired was a fate not known to Julien Sorel, but which Lucien Leuwen shared with the hero of *Armance,* Octave de Malivert. The thematic connection with impotence would be hard to miss, though clearly the moral impotence of Lucien, debilitated by wealth that was symptomatic of a political malaise, gave the novelist greater scope than the very special plight of the doomed, high-minded hero of his first extended fiction. Just the same, Lucien, wryly taken in hand for his mother's sake by his witty omnipotent father (a great banker in an age ruled by gold), had to leave his mother's salon and strike out on his own if ever he was to be able to call himself a man.

Exile to Nancy as a lieutenant in the 27th Lancers regiment was the cure, and it effected not much more than the demonstration that the youth was no more at home amid the morose vulgarity of garrison life than he had been, as a serious-minded pampered ex-chemist, amid the empty compliments and ever-watchful vanities of salon habitués. The landscape around him was barren: café life, provincial amenities, oafish and resentful fellow officers, endless virtuous jeremiads from the honest journalist Gauthier, the leader of the republican opposition. Lucien shielded himself against the insolence of his colleagues by an ostentatious display of domestics in livery and the consumption of expensive champagne. Having thus earned as a fop the respect his genuine merit could not command, Lucien ended by breaching the jealously guarded preserves of the reactionary aristocracy, under the guidance of the eloquent hunchback Dr. Du Poirier, called in to dress a wound sustained in a duel. Young Leuwen's fine horsemanship, his Parisian high breeding, his wit and good looks soon conciliated the fervent backers of Henri V—and he exchanged the drivel of the billiard room for the antics of "those country comedians," the troglodytic partisans of an uncompromising return to feudal privilege and the divine right of kings. Invariably as the name Louis-Philippe came up, one of the gentlemen would bark: *Thief!* and up to ten times a day the whole noble assemblage would roar with laughter. Lucien could hardly believe his ears.

That he owed his fine reception by those titled buffoons at least in part to his accomplished horsemanship was jest enough in itself, for a fall from horseback suffered under the window of the beautiful Mme de Chasteller, on the day of his arrival in Nancy, was what impelled him to seek their society in the first place. Lucien *fell* from horseback as one is said to *fall* in love: his weakness, in the game of love, was to be his only strength. To strut before a lovely woman was an accomplishment open to the run of fine horsemen that constituted her circle of acquaintances. To be felled by his mount at first glimpse of her face was the mark of a man smitten, of a man both unwary of the unknown god and capable of sustaining a mystic wound.

The innocence of Parsifal, in fact his ineptness, came to be Lucien's own passport into that land of the unknown where his salvation lay. More so than any other Stendhalian hero he was vulnerable: neither Fabrizio's high birth nor Julien's guerrilla mentality shielded him against the sense of personal failure attendant on his easy circumstances and overmatched practical sense. The sole example of the son of an affectionate father in the gallery of Stendhal's major creations, Lucien Leuwen paid for his good fortune with a heightened sense of his personal inadequacy: "What miracles my father would have accomplished in my place ... in a conversation like this directed toward one person, but to be understood by another!" (*Green Huntsman*, 289) was his quite standard reaction in his finest hour, when the appearance of flirting with the reigning beauty, Madame d'Hocquincourt, in Mme de Chasteller's hearing, gave him the means of breaking down for good the latter's pretended indifference. Falling from horseback—as he was to do a second time, when a stirring of the curtain gave him to think he was being watched from the fateful window, to which he daily returned—thus took the measure accurately of the humility required of the hapless servant of the god.

Of all the obstacles that stood in the path of his love, his own revulsion at the thought of a state so far removed from virtuous dedication to the public weal turned out to be the least. "Playing at cup-and-ball by the mouth of a volcano" was the inelegant image by which he vainly sought to shake himself out of his culpable moonings: the grave, dreamy eyes of Mme de Chasteller easily prevailed against such feeble remonstrations. They prevailed, in fact, against the slanders of all Nancy, irked by her absentminded aloofness, which falsely persuaded Lucien from the first that a lieutenant-colonel had previously melted her indifference, and that his greatest failing in her eyes came of his lowly military rank. Though she was in fact as chaste as her name implied, Mme de Chasteller acquired in his mind's eye a heartless, frivolous double whose worst exertions were powerless to exorcise the overwhelming truth of her artless presence and of her unplumbed gaze.

Her great wealth had caused Mme de Chasteller, the young widow of a man many times her age, once the ornament of the court of Charles X, to be practically immured in Nancy by her father, the grasping Marquis de Pontlevé, fearful of another popular uprising and anxious to spend the next emigration in moneyed ease. Her character did nothing to relieve her solitude: she rejóiced in it, in fact, since "daydreaming was her supreme pleasure . . .," a pensiveness which fed, not on the little preoccupations of money and prestige which her circle thought supreme, but on the sight of a pitiful old beggarwoman, which escaped them altogether. Yet such conventional trappings of moral and physical captivity as the ill-will of her acquaintances, who felt snubbed by her remoteness and baffled by her character, the watchfulness of her tyrannical father—the officiousness of the evil dwarf Du Poirier, adding to it all its Niebelungen touch—did little to impede the progress of love. Du Poirier, in fact, was indirectly the occasion of bringing Lucien within whispering distance of the *ferne Geliebte:* for within sight of her grave beautiful eyes to whisper was all the mortified youth could do, so bereft was he of all the advantages that had made him the ornament of Nancy's most brilliant soirées.

Speechless at the side of the beloved, Lucien unknowingly conjured away his worst enemy: the fear on Bathilde's part that he was a Parisian *roué* bent on adding another to his string of conquests. For such was to be the comedy of errors that was to keep the two lovers apart: while he struggled with the unlikely image of her as coquette, she, poor deluded soul, thought *him* a Don Juan and (the mask he had adopted to enter her circle) a fop. Emboldened by his poor countenance, she thawed him into speech, only to discover that he could speak well and from the heart, that he spoke to her in fact

with that shade of delicate familiarity permissible between kindred souls when they meet and recognize each other in the midst of the masks of that ignoble masquerade called society. Thus might two angels address each other if, having descended from heaven on some mission, they should meet here below. (184)

The ice was thus broken with an abruptness that left them both disoriented. The distance was too great between the two worlds in which they were called upon to draw breath almost simultaneously: the unreflecting abandon of the heights, where they stood wholly disclosed to one another, bereft of all caution and propriety, and the stifling conventionalities within which a well-bred pair, newly introduced, must perforce confine their incipient familiarity.

The consciousness of her warm and unguarded response to Lucien's artless declaration led Bathilde de Chasteller into ecstasies of gloom: she had forfeited all right to her self-respect and to his consideration! The coldness with which she later sought to repair such a disaster merely plunged the inexperienced Lucien into despair: he had not the practiced eye needed to read the state of inner disarray she sought to conceal. Had he had the wit, as he sat under her window in the gloom of night, to summon such a felicitous phrase as: " 'Good evening, Madam. Won't you deign to make a sign that I am heard?' . . . Madame de Chasteller would probably have whispered: 'Goodnight, M. Leuwen.' And the intonation of those three words could have left nothing to be desired by the most exigent lover" (212).

The occasional informality of provincial life (the other side of the coin of its heavy-handedness) was to prove the solvent of these agonies. Bathilde and Lucien could meet in the relaxed, familiar climate of the Serpierre household, amid numerous ungainly marriageable daughters. The suggestion was made that they form a party to ride to the Green Huntsman, an outdoor café kept by Germans in the woods on the outskirts of town, where music played of an evening. In that enchanting setting, with Mozart sounding in the distance and the calm of the woods surrounding them, their love reached its meditative fullness, beyond pride and beyond speech. The utter sincerity of Lucien's protestations found its echo in Bathilde's unquestioning acceptance of them. Although remorse and self-mistrust could do them further mischief, "sincerity, music, and great forests" (231) had sealed an intimacy that was proof against their vacillations. As the *Charterhouse* was to embody Stendhal's Italian dream, *Lucien Leuwen,* as is manifest from the consonance of the hero's name and the Eastern border locale of its major episode, captured the spirit of his German adventure. The Green Huntsman Kaffeehaus, with its celebration of green nature, its peaceful woods resounding to Mozart, executed on the horn by players from Bohemia, caught up the slow, dreamy rhythm of that idyllic Germany celebrated by Mme de Staël, with its train of philosophers, musicians, placid burghers, and ingenuous maidens.[6]

The Germanic straightforwardness of the two lovers, whose inexperience allowed them to unpack their hearts practically at first sight of one another, was matched by their indecisiveness. Too much lost in the sensation of the moment, Lucien never traveled the road from intimacy to consummation. But then *Lucien Leuwen, roman inachevé,* was also, in the English sense, to be the novel of *non-achievement.* Neither the military urgency of Julien's blueprint for conquest, nor the threat of poison hanging over Fabrizio in the Farnese tower, came to the aid of a hero so overmatched by his own father that he was "convinced that he had no gift for making himself desirable to a woman *(faire vouloir une femme),* especially when he was seriously in love with her" (264-65). Love and politics interweave in Stendhal's novels as they do in Racine's plays: in a regime where a man of character, for want even of enemies to strike down, could not *get anywhere,* no tension from the political scene could be counted on to energize the too considerate lovers. Hence Dr. Du Poirier, the evil genius who had brought them together, had to take a hand to drive them asunder. In answer to the sullen resentment of the noblemen under his guidance, the political commissar for the legitimist cause in Nancy undertook to extirpate from their midst the servant of the upstart Louis-Philippe, who threatened to walk off with their most beautiful heiress. A sinister comedy was staged by the doctor, called to Bathilde's bedside for a minor ailment: a pretended delivery, within hearing of Lucien, closeted in the house by a complaisant servant. The horrified Leuwen galloped back to Paris, home to his mother, closing on a note of defeat an angelic vision that had not found the means to turn itself into an earthly reality.

Faced with the return of an incorrigibly serious-minded son, François Leuwen first applied a mild regimen of occupational therapy to build up the lad's damaged standing (as an abruptly-retired cavalry man), while leaving him no time for senseless brooding. His career in the Ministry of the Interior, supplemented by regular attendance at the Opera, promised, by sheer exhaustion, to keep him off all thoughts of suicide. An unceremonious integrity, which effected the discomfiture of some fairly influential personages, led to a campaign of whispers taxing young Leuwen with Saint-Simonian convictions. So drastic an accusation, rendered plausible by his earnest turn of mind, called for more drastic counter-measures. Lucien Leuwen was required by his father to display a passionate attachment for an actress. Fearful of success, which would force him to betray the fidelity he had sworn in his heart to the faithless Mme de Chasteller, Lucien wrung from his father permission to court a woman of virtue (an alternative the banker was much amused to see deemed less risky!). Mme Grandet, the reigning beauty of the *juste-milieu* regime, a blonde whose complexion rivaled that of a German maiden, a woman moreover of spotless reputation, thus came to be chosen as the object of his official devotion. She was in every way calculated to repel him. There was in her neither tenderness nor true greatness of spirit. Wealthy, beautiful, gifted, and admired, she quailed at her want of birth or title, and sought, by a remorseless display of *ideas,* to usurp the intellectual sovereignty of a Mme de Staël. This essentially vulgar and heartless beauty did not long remain indifferent to the honor of plunging into despair so creditable a young man as the young M. Leuwen. The banker-deputy, his father, was in fact summoned by her to an interview, of which the net effect was to gain Lucien a victory the banker paid for with the nomination of her husband to the Ministry.

The sacrifice of Mme Grandet was perhaps no more ruthless than had been the treatment of that other plebeian beauty hankering after birth,

Mme de Fervaques; but Stendhal certainly allowed it to be more complete. To the odiousness of her bargain he had the unkindness to add a genuine infatuation. Lucien won her heart by that quality that had never been allowed to cross her gaze: his utter lack of affectation (his *naturel*). Unfortunately for her, the banker's tact, for once, had failed him—and Lucien became aware that his first amorous conquest had been negotiated for by Leuwen *père*. Faithful to the maxim of inflicting no unnecessary pain,[7] young Leuwen remained kind, but the lady henceforth swooned in vain. The sudden death of his father, bringing in its wake financial ruin, spared Lucien the pain of further rigor. Mme de Chasteller's faithful swain could ride to Italy unencumbered. The parody of love had not so much as chipped a heart inured to its real presence.

III *The Vow*

Love thrives on prohibitions. In Italy, a land of archaic social and political arrangements, arbitrary enough to nurture passionate resentments in the bosom of a volatile and energetic people, it would never lack for the kind of naked contradiction that exacerbated preference into irresistible passion. The unfinished *Lucien Leuwen* looked beyond its Nordic stasis toward a resolution in that Southern clime. But the task of setting forth Stendhal's epiphany, his enchanted discovery of the landscape of his own soul, was reserved for a greater novel, triumphantly dashed off in seven weeks of incessant writing, dictation, and correction: *The Charterhouse of Parma.*

Julien Sorel had been, in effect, a motherless hero. Lucien Leuwen had sought refuge in the wilds of Nancy from the perfection of a filial love that threatened to unman him, and he had found the Princess of his reward in that faraway land. Fabrizio del Dongo was presumably the son of that Lieutenant (later encountered on the battlefield of Waterloo as General) Robert, who was billeted in the palace of the ungallantly stranded Marchesa. He was to match this double parentage by a duplication that was far less common. His aunt Gina Pietranera, later Duchessa Sanseverina, and in the end Contessa Mosca, stood by the side of the Marchesa as a second, far more active and influential mother to the boy, a mother who could, without excessive scandal, nurture for him incestuous longings that raised love, from the first, to the pitch of incipient tragedy.

Gina Pietranera had the daring, the wit, the beauty, the generosity of spirit required of the lady of a hero's dreams. She had married the dashing impecunious Pietranera against the wishes of her brother, the mean-spirited reactionary Marchese del Dongo. She had retired with a good grace to the fourth floor to which her early widowhood (and her miserly brother's unforgiveness) relegated her—and whither all Milan speedily repaired. She had openly spurned the wealthy fashionable Limercati, who had declined to avenge with a few pistol shots Pietranera's death in a rigged duel. She zealously watched over the fate of the volunteer for Waterloo, whose cause she had embraced *con brio*. When that splendid youth made his appearance in Parma, after serving the standard apprenticeship of respectability enjoined by his well-counseled protectress—daily attendance at mass, avoidance of all appearance of wit or thought, the open courting of a noble mistress—an apprenticeship that had been capped by enrollment at the seminary in Naples, the innocent love born of physical and spiritual kinship took on an added dimension, which sent a brief shudder down Mosca's spine, and soon gave Fabrizio himself an inkling that strange perils lurked.

Conte Mosca had fallen in love with Gina on a visit to Milan, when the all-powerful Prime Minister of Parma had been struck first with her beauty, then, as she held court in her box at La Scala, with her wit and character. Fearless, unillusioned, and above all disinterested (though a prime minister, he had no fortune to offer her!), Mosca was to be the proof that in the court of love age can be no bar, when a youthful freshness smooths its wrinkled brow. Before knocking on the door of her box the Conte shook as he had not since his twenties; such timidity in a man who had, moreover, the good grace to laugh at his eminence in Lilliputian Parma, served him better than both looks and fortune. Mosca earned the right to watch over the exiled Fabrizio, as Gina removed to Parma married off to an elderly Duke, overjoyed to represent his land at a faraway court, while under his nominal spouse the palazzo Sanseverina turned into the brilliant center of a city rescued from gloom.

The game of love, as befits the land of both Petrarch and Aretino, had thus become infinitely complicated. The elder Leuwen watching with mocking paternal affection over the apple of a beloved wife's eye, had given some intimation of an Œdipal trio, in which the father wryly worked in with Nature's unfathomable plan. A far deadlier contest appeared in the offing here, where natural ties were wanting to soften the conflict of youth and age, or even to remove the chance of a quasi-incestuous regression. Prince Ernesto-Ranuce IV did his poisonous best to kindle the discord by an anonymous letter, which drove the distracted Mosca to the thoughts of stabbing the too handsome Fabrizio under the eyes of his unthinkingly adoring Duchessa.

All three were as honorable as they were passionate, however, and neither violence nor treachery needed to come into play. Though Gina remained blessedly unconscious of the quality of her solicitude for her handsome young kinsman, Fabrizio soon became aware that between his aunt and the Conte he risked playing the part of *terzo incomodo*, swelling the party into a crowd. The unsettling thought arose in his mind that sooner or later the Duchessa might stumble upon the truth of her own feelings, that he would be confronted with the alternative of black ingratitude or feigning a passion he could not feel. The unlovely role of *casto Giuseppe,* virtuous young Joseph chastely repulsing the advances of Potiphar's wife, promised to mingle nastiness with ridicule: altogether, an unappealing prospect.

His inability to respond to the divine Sanseverina's half-discovered passion persuaded Fabrizio that he suffered from the failing which every Stendhalian hero (before he is disabused by experience) bemoans in himself to some degree: an incapacity to feel anything approaching that much-vaunted state called love. The boredom he had endured in Naples courting a duchess who had not been unkind helped to implant a conviction that freed him of remorse in his unresponsiveness to Gina. Fabrizio, in consequence, took up with a young actress, to fill the void of his stony heart, and give himself an occupation unconnected with the Duchessa. He succeeded beyond his wildest dreams in exorcising his peril. The infuriated Giletti, little Marietta Valserra's amorous impresario, rushed at him with sword and pistol, in the open countryside, where Fabrizio had been overseeing an excavation, and lost his life in the scuffle. Fabrizio could now, as well as in Milan, boast outlawry in Parma, where the Prince, eager to humiliate the too-independent Duchessa, inflated manslaughter in self-defense into a crime of state, punishable by twenty years in a prison fortress.

A refugee now from his adoptive home, Fabrizio resumed the underground existence forced upon him once before by the denunciation of his brother Ascanio. Under the alias of Joseph Bossi, the former barometer salesman led a relatively retired life in Bologna, alternating a domestic tranquility with Marietta that quite failed to induce the well-known ecstasies of the passion that eluded him, with the sport of stealing the great singer Fausta from the jealous count who held her sequestered. It was from such pastimes that he was snatched away by a note in Gina's handwriting forged at the behest of Marchesa Raversi, to land in chains at the foot of Parma's infamous Farnese Tower. His gaze encountered there the angelic Clelia, moments after he had struck down the insolent Barbone, a clerk bold enough to bully a man who seemed fallen from grace, though a lord of the land and a del Dongo!

Fabrizio came out of the office escorted by three constables; they were taking him to the room which had been allotted to him. Clelia looked out of the window, the prisoner was quite close to her. At that moment she answered her father's question in the words: *"I will go with you."*

Fabrizio, hearing these words uttered close to his ear, raised his eyes and met the girl's gaze. He was struck, especially, by the expression of melancholy on her face. "How she was improved," he thought, "since our meeting near Como! What an air of profound thought! . . . They are quite right to compare her with the Duchessa; what angelic features!" Barbone, the blood-stained clerk, who had not taken his stand beside the carriage without a purpose, held up his hand . . . and, moving round behind the carriage until he reached the window next which the General was sitting:

"As the prisoner has committed an act of violence in the interior of the citadel," he said to him, "in consideration of Article 157 of the regulations, would it not be as well to put the handcuffs on him for three days?"

"Go to the devil!" cried the General, still considerably embarrassed by the arrest . . . .

During this brief dialogue, Fabrizio stood superb among the group of constables, his expression was certainly the proudest and most noble that one could imagine; his fine and delicate features, and the contemptuous smile that strayed over his lips made a charming contrast with the coarse appearance of the constables who stood round him. But all this formed, so to speak, only the external part of his physiognomy; he was enraptured by the heavenly beauty of Clelia, and his eye betrayed his surprise to the full. She, profoundly pensive, had never thought of drawing back her head from the window; he bowed to her with a half-smile of the utmost respect; then, after a moment's silence:

"It seems to me, Signorina," he said to her, "that, once before, near a lake, I had the honour of meeting you, in the company of the police?"

Clelia blushed, and was so taken aback that she could find no words in which to reply. "What a noble air among all these coarse creatures," she had been saying to herself at the moment when Fabrizio spoke to her. The profound pity, we might almost say the tender emotion in which she was plunged deprived her of the presence of mind necessary to find words, no matter what; she became conscious of her silence and blushed all the deeper. At this moment the bolts of the great gate of the citadel were drawn back with a clang; had not his Excellency's carriage been waiting for at least a minute? The echo was so loud in this vaulted passage that even if Clelia had found something to say in reply Fabrizio could not have caught her words.

Borne away by the horses which had broken into a gallop immediately after crossing the drawbridge, Clelia said to herself: "He must have thought me very silly!" Then suddenly she added: "Not only silly; he must have felt that I had a base nature, he must have thought that I did not respond to his greeting because he is a prisoner and I am the governor's daughter." (271-73)

What incomparable surroundings a prison makes for the epiphany of love! A proud and noble youth in chains, a malevolent jailer covered with blood, clanking bolts, vaulted passages, a carriage drawn away at a gallop silencing the pensive heavenly maiden, overcome with the shame of being the warden's daughter and of seeming to despise a fallen courtly foe . . . . For it was love, of course, which had caught up with Fabrizio at last in the apparition that cast a ray of melancholy beauty on the grim drama of his incarceration. She was the girl who nearly shared his carriage, when General Conti, then out of favor, had been apprehended between Como and Milan, after Fabrizio himself had narrowly missed being taken in his stead. "She would be a charming prison companion," he had thought at the time. "What profound thought she has behind that brow! She would know how to love" (88). The Salzburg bough had every chance to grow its wreath of diamonds: the pensive maiden, in a very real sense, *had* turned into a prison companion.

Parma and its deadly intrigues, the Duchessa and her paralyzing affection were far, far below, at the foot of the immense tower where Fabrizio in solitary confinement devised an alphabet of love, to exchange spelled-out greetings with the girl at the aviary window. While Mosca, Gina, and eventually Clelia herself, converted by the fear that he would be poisoned, took every risk and mobilized immense resources to engineer his escape, Fabrizio, as had Julien before him, tasted the heavenly release of a solitude whose every moment could be devoted to his innocent love. Clelia both close and far away, spoken to brokenly but espied unseen in the touching routine of a sequestered maiden, belonged to her captive admirer with an immediacy, and yet a purity, which freedom and bodily possession would not have preserved. The captive body, once more, had released the soul from its cares, to dwell wholly in a dream which no admixture of imperfect reality could mar.

Never again was Fabrizio to taste such unmixed bliss, not even in his brief possession of Clelia's body and soul, in the course of his second captivity, on the day that the plot to poison him had made her break into his cell, in defiance of her own safety and reputation. Immurement in his prison tower had vouchsafed an interlude of perfect peace in a life buffeted by the passions of others. Gina's despairing jealousy was to seal Clelia's marriage to the Marchese Crescenzi. Clelia's betrayal of the murderous Fabbio Conti led to unending guilt, expiated in her consent to an odious marriage and in the vow taken to the Madonna never to look again on Fabrizio's face. The hapless coadjutor took to preaching sermons fired with the eloquence of his despair, of which the fame soon betrayed the beloved into spellbound attendance, and a modified observance of her vow. Years of furtive lovemaking culminated in Fabrizio's kidnapping of his own son, whose untimely death Clelia did not survive. Archbishop del Dongo, having resigned his see, retired to die a monk in the charterhouse of Parma.

In Italy, the land of the dream, love quickly flared to the passionate and murderous intensity Stendhal had admiringly chronicled in "The Abbess of Castro" and its sequel of Quattrocento tales. The gentle Clelia turned tigress in defense of the threatened life of the man she loved in defiance of all reason (for she firmly believed him Gina's lover). A villainous death, perpetual incarceration, inextricable vows hedged the course of felicity with the kind of dire perilousness unknown in tamer climes. The machinations of buffoons put men of spirit under the shade of torture, exile, and clanking chains with quite the same effect as might saner or grander schemes. Gina had to prostitute herself, Clelia marry a fool, Fabrizio conceal a lover's heart beneath the episcopal robes of a saint. The setting might be *opera buffa:* the horror and the bliss were intensely real.

The hero of *The Charterhouse of Parma* sums up in his fate all that his author envied and deplored in the Italy to which, in his epitaph, he pronounced himself reborn, as Arrigo Beyle, *Milanese.* Political disaster stalked any man worthy of the name, even before he could set his hand to a task that might help unshackle his fellow countrymen. But the very quality that left him little hope of survival promised him to a rarer fate: the shared solitude of the very best, of the *happy few*—Conte Mosca, Gina Pietranera, Clelia Conti—soaring in the heavens of loving disinterestedness, caring one for the other with an abandon not known to beings less eccentric and less imperiled, subject solely to the gentle tyranny of love.

IV Donne ch'avete intelletto d'Amore

Armance, the title heroine of the first novel Stendhal wrote, earned our esteem and the hero's love by the coolness with which she greeted that erstwhile friend, on the day that his fortune rose to a figure in the millions. In a salon crowded with fawning dignitaries, Armance de Zohiloff, the ruined daughter of a Russian nobleman, though reduced to play the part of a poor relation, alone had the pride to withhold her admiration from a man turned wealthy overnight. For

that young woman was of a singular character . . . . Under an exterior of perfect gentleness, Mlle de Zohiloff concealed a firmness of will to match the harsh climate of her childhood . . . . Scarcely 18, she had already endured fairly uncommon misfortunes. Hence the reason, perhaps, that life's little events seemed to glide on her soul without moving her. Sometimes it was possible to read in her glance that she could feel intensely, but it could be seen that nothing vulgar could touch her . . . . She had acquired the habit of judging herself with little regard for the effect she made on others, but with much concern for her own feelings today, of which the memory might tomorrow be the bane of her life . . . . None of her actions bore directly on the exaggerated notion of what a woman owes to herself, and yet a charm made up of grace and heavenly restraint pervaded her whole person. (*Romans*, Pléiade, I, 53-57)

The portrait of the beloved, as she appears in subsequent Stendhalian novels, stands fully revealed in this very first sketch. Her pride is genuine, hence she has no thought of being overbearing. Gentle, serene, remote—she has the slightly exotic appearance of a creature from another world, or more accurately: from another sphere. She scarcely understands the language of self-interest which alone is spoken in the exalted social and political circles where fate has cast her lot: hence the enforced retreat into a beloved solitude, where vulgar claims and boasts never intrude. Her serenity, which arises from disdain for a world of greed and self-importance, is not to be mistaken for softness. Stendhal, who at 22 wrote in his journal (January 7, 1805): "None but a woman of high mettle could make me happy," never shared in the nineteenth century's worship of woman's frailty. Steely determination in the service of a passion set in motion by her true interests—the interests of the heart—was to be, early and late, the mark of the Stendhalian heroine. The retiring nature of Clelia Conti, the painful reserve of Bathilde de Chasteller scarcely encourage the willingness to cast reputation to the winds when the occasion demands it: the more striking their calm resolve—to say nothing of Mme de Rênal's unbridled recklessness, openly trysting with her would-be assassin in sight of all Besançon and Verrières.

Stendhal is that rarity among great writers—as Beyle was among men: the man who both loves women and esteems them. His women are neither men *manqués* (except when they rejoice in false pride, as do Mmes Grandet and de Fervaques), nor sweet nonentities ripe for the plucking. (No pedestals are in sight, nor any wilting camellias!) They are fit companions for a hero: high-minded, free of false cares, melting in love and fierce in contention. Their models are the fearless ladies whose desperate struggle for happiness was carried on against the bloodiest odds, as chronicled in the popular tales Stendhal was to immortalize under the title *Chroniques italiennes*. The loss of his young mother, whom he remembered as beautiful, lively, and gay; the exalted character of his great-aunt Elisabeth Gagnon; the resonance he found for his tough-minded teachings in his younger sister Pauline, upon whom he urged all the philosophy at his command, may have helped him shape such uncommon views. The happy circumstance of an ardent temperament refracted in a cool mind, at all events, allowed him to absorb Rousseau's wholesome rejection of the pampered female without succumbing to his rantings against the superior woman. Romantic in his worship of the dream, he was too much the child of the eighteenth century not to insist that the dream also come true. The enchanting vision, in his novels, is made flesh and blood. At that point the promise of inaccessible beauty is redeemed by character. Nobility of mind, genuineness of feeling fill out the vague silhouette held out to romantic yearning. A woman is born, worthy in every point of the immensity of our undefined expectations.

The hero's release in love is not simply effected, therefore, by an encounter with *das ewig Weibliche*. Another being, equally vulnerable, equally high-minded, possessed of a character, a personality, a set of class and family prejudices of her own, meets him in this terra incognita, unknown, in fact, to them both. The *I* of the book encounters another *I*, neither to be swallowed by the other.

The ultimate expression of this rare impartiality was Stendhal's determination to write a novel whose hero is a woman. An 1830 novella, *Mina de Vanghel,* recast into the beginning of a novel, *Le Rose et le Vert (The Rose and the Green),* around 1837, and the unfinished novel *Lamiel* (1839) testify to the writer's preoccupation with the possibility of such a transposition. In the first two works, a Prussian heiress arrives in Paris, determined to live her own life free of cant and fortune hunters. In the crush of dandies and intrigues, the first man she meets whose straightforwardness matches her own impels the fearless Mina de Vanghel to enter his wife's employ as a seamstress, whereupon Alfred de Larçay soon returns her love. To revenge herself on that lady's "slanderous" accusations—she had called her an adventuress—Mina embroils Madame de Larçay in a fictitious love affair with a count, hot in the pursuit of Mina's millions; she then alerts the husband through anonymous letters, which brings on a duel followed by eight months of flawless happiness. When the gentleman learns that his marriage had been broken up by such brazen tactics, he leaves her in a huff. " 'Such are the risks to which great souls are exposed, but they have their own recourse,' thought Mina, as she walked to the window and followed her lover's progress to the end of the street. When he was out of sight, she went to Alfred's room and put a bullet through her heart." (*Romans,* II, 1174)

To account for a manly directness and the total absence of affectation he wished for in his heroine, Stendhal made Mina a German Protestant. To produce the same character from native stock he had to make Lamiel a foundling, brought up in a Norman village by a beadle-turned-schoolteacher and his wife—the worthy couple having taken that means to disinherit their dangerously free-thinking nephew (suspected of armed resistance to the Prussian invaders during the restoration of the Bourbons in 1815!). Lively, curious, and gay, the girl discovers the freedom and adventurousness of life in a few forbidden books (the *Aeneid!*—and the lives of two celebrated highwaymen, Mandrin and Cartouche). The naysaying of her childhood, hedged in with rebuke and admonition soon appears to her in its true light: the beadle might be kind, but he isn't very bright! Nor is he generous, like Cartouche, nor half as brave! In sum, her parents are to be felt sorry for, certainly not obeyed or admired! Taken to the local chateau to be a reader and companion for an aging duchess (wit and liveliness have their reward in the age of *ennui,* as Julien Sorel had already demonstrated), Lamiel becomes the apple of that woman's eye, while the ambitious hunchback doctor Sansfin[8] lavishes upon her his cynical wisdom, as he hopes to make of her the main lever of his future power. Caught between her own ignorance of the world and her eagerness to make sense of it in the light of the mind-cleansing principles learned from the entertainingly wicked doctor, Lamiel turns her sharpened faculties to the solution of that enigma, everywhere spoken of but so far unknown to her: love. She talks a young dolt into "taking her to the woods": when this merely results in his losing his post as assistant schoolmaster, she *bribes* him into livelier intercourse. "Is there no more to it than that?" she is then led to inquire.

Elopement with the young duke, the son of her protectress, fails to turn that timid youth into a man of action. Talk of waistcoats striped gray on gray in turn fails to secure for the young man the intimacy of a girl who rejoices in the power to shake his silly composure. Leaving him stranded in Rouen, she dashes to Paris with all his money, to become the mistress of a ruined young count, whose pose she mistakes for genuine *insouciance.* The novel ends as she gives herself to a rival of the count, on condition the count is made to learn how openly she makes light of him: "I take you," she said, "so that I can laugh openly at the count and see him develop his character." *(New Directions,* 251) Among the alternative endings sketched in by Stendhal, two at least make Lamiel fall in love with a murderer, who is also a thief, whose execution she avenges in one case by burning down the court building. "What she liked in that quite unsightly man was that he did not strain while in repose, being sure to find himself when the time came for action." *(Romans,* II, 1036)

While every feature of his uninhibited heroines was a stab at the heart of nineteenth-century prudery and propriety, Stendhal clearly took them to heart for more than their shock value. Mina is not resigned to settle into a comfortably vapid existence as the mistress of a "Doll's House"; Lamiel has no intention of figuring as the prize of some fop's possessions. Both repudiate the passivity that is the lot of their sex, not out of some empty wish to settle a score with the opposite sex, or to bring down the walls of masculine privilege, but to exercise a choice of destiny and satisfy their legitimate curiosity as to their true place in the scheme of things. A lively mind, a firm will, a stout heart are not, to Stendhal, the natural endowment belonging to one sex alone. In their absence, beauty itself could be no more than vapid. Vergil's Camilla, the heroines of Tasso, Rousseau's Julie herself had served to keep alive a worthier ideal of woman. The Abbess of Castro, Beatrix Cenci, in his own tales, had held high the torch of heroism in an age of lawless passion. The beloved of Julien Sorel, of Lucien Leuwen, of Fabrizio del Dongo each reveal hidden treasures of resolution, unsuspected from the gentle diffidence of their womanly ways (theirs is not the more quarrelsome virtue of a Gina or a Mathilde!) Mina and Lamiel resort to manly daring in order to secure that right to happiness which, rightly conceived, is the highest imperative for a superior being: the happiness of giving herself to one whose own freedom from pettiness and deceit marks him out as her heroic counterpart. The terra incognita of love beckons to man and woman alike, provided only that they have the grace and the daring to lose themselves in another. Honor, reputation are not for them perishable possessions, fastened upon them by the consent of a fretful public. Heedlessness in the service of the purest joy, and heedlessness alone, marks the servants of the god, the noble company of *the happy few* worthy to love, worthy of love.

CHAPTER 3

The Bog

P*LAT* is an adjective that does heavy duty in the Stendhalian corpus. Rendered variously as *flat, stale, low,* it describes fairly tellingly the human landscape against which the hero pits his exertions—which remain, consequently, quite beyond the grasp or even the interest of his bemused contemporaries. The bog-lands of human experience beckon to all those whose greed, thick-headedness, or self-regard cut them off from the upward surge of true ambition. Theirs the safe inglorious paths of flat horizontality—leaving it to the *happy few* to streak the heavens with the meteor rise and fall of a doomed undertaking. Capital is lovingly accumulated, power slowly gathered, rank steadily scaled by these patient trudgers, as the hero speeds to the scaffold or the charterhouse: the kingdom, and the power, and the glory are firmly locked in their ignoble hands, while God's elect soar naked into their reward of a higher happiness.

Stendhal, unlike Balzac, was unmoved by the heady appeal of money and power. He had had a whiff of the one and the other in his balmy Napoleonic days, and perhaps he made a trifle too much of the disinterestedness with which he turned down a post "worth millions" under the Restoration. Brought up on expectations of plenty which under the penurious stewardship of his luckless father failed to materialize, his disappointment took the form of a superiority to his niggardly fortune, which tallied with his need to renounce Chérubin Beyle and all his works. His own impracticality was vindicated by the failure of a practical-minded father who had kept him on short rations to further bootless speculations. A military half-pension supplemented by a small legacy, together with his free-lance work in the English periodicals, kept him supplied with the small comforts he required from life, under the Restoration: café dining, the theater and the opera, suitable clothes for salon attendance. A minor diplomatic post kept body alive and his soul unencumbered under the July monarchy. Yet far more to the point than the commendable decency of the man is the remarkable consistency his life exhibited with the dictates of his imagination. Balzac, in life, was constantly intoxicated by the prospect of millions he never made, but his intoxication carried through in his breathless recreation of the sordid excitement of a fortune made and undone in grain speculation or the manipulation of real estate: Gobseck, Nucingen, Grandet, thanks to him, are names to conjure with. Stendhal's relative disdain for the glitter of hard cash or gold braid consigns the romance of capitalism in his novels, along with its honor guard of state officialdom, to the low ground of comedy, purified by healthy gusts of laughter. The Church and the high nobility are thrown in for good measure, as relics of a past that goes on turning a deaf ear to the news of its own demise.

Early and late in the novels, from *Armance,* in fact, to *Lamiel,* the hero's high destiny is shown ludicrously at cross purposes with the often well-wishing mob of those who see no farther than their purses, whose whole occupation indeed is "to get their share of the Budget"! Octave de Malivert, in *Armance,* owes his sudden eminence in the salons to the passage of a bill to compensate émigré families for the loss of their colossal fortunes. He is alone to blush at the spoliation. Armance's coolness to his success assures the young lady in waiting of his heart. And Lamiel must likewise shake off the preachments, though kindly meant, of her dunderheaded foster parents, if she is not to remain, like themselves, forever on her knees before wealth and position. A look at the world of the three major novels will help us sort out the ubiquitous array of *interests* and pretensions that serve to portray the contemporary scene, in the eyes of one little disposed to cheer on the side of mediocrity, in what he called *la chasse au bonheur.*

I *Verrières, Besançon, Paris*

In the small town of Verrières, where Julien Sorel first dreams of Napoleonic glory, the rule of self-interest knows no shame. It is exhibited nakedly in the self-satisfied countenance of the nobleman-mayor, in the hearty effrontery of the poorhouse director Valenod, in the mean, piercing glance of *père* Sorel's little gray eyes. The first sight that comes into view is the picturesque stream, the Doubs, harnessed to the mechanical saw run by Sorel senior; in the town proper, a deafening sound of hammer blows gives notice that a large manufacture of nails, powered from the same waters, sustains the fortunes of the mayor of the town, M. de Rênal, who owes to this same eye- (and ear-) sore the profits that paid for his handsome stone townhouse, surrounded by its extensive wall-enclosed terraced gardens. The relation of beauty to profit is all at once made doubly clear. What escapes our glance is the tale that must be further unfolded: Sorel's sawmill had to be moved downhill at great cost to the mayor's purse and pride, to make room for an enlargement of those grandiose gardens. Since vanity is ever a poor match for avarice, the stubborn old peasant got the best of that bargain. Julien's own rise as Latin tutor to the Rênal children is to be an episode in that uneven contest, which it raised to a level beyond the comprehension of either contestant.

The older Sorel gives up his upland site for a better one on the riverbank four times the size, plus a six thousand franc cash payment. The deal faithfully mirrors the man. Hard, secretive, brutally contemptuous of what escapes his narrow focus (like that delicate younger son of his, who wastes his time on *books),* he is the successful peasant become small entrepreneur, ready to turn, with infinite patience and infinite watchfulness, the faraway corner into the petty bourgeoisie. His ways have the toughness and the occasional violence of a class not far removed from the brutalities of barnyard existence (the slap that sends Julien sprawling is certainly the latest in a long line of beatings); a class, moreover, firmly kept "in its place" by the combined weight and power of the whole of society. Hence the relief with which Julien escapes from the blows and the hatred which had been his lot under that unrelenting master, to pit his small strength against more tractable foes. Hence also the sole shiver of unreasoned terror he is to feel, in his prison cell, at the thought of his father's visit. Fortunately for him, he bethinks himself of the saving phrase: *j'ai fait des économies!* (I have money set aside). At Verrières, even a dragon can be stared down, provided you carry some cash.

The poorhouse director Valenod takes us only one rung up the scale. His character is pure brass. Loud, self-seeking, and vain (he's had his eye on Mme de Rênal, much to that lady's unfeigned embarrassment), his scandalous mishandling of the funds for the poor even manages to bring down the visit of an inspector from the Paris ministry (the first event of the novel). Needless to say, the inspection merely costs Father Chélan his curacy (in his 80th year), for having had the audacity to take the inspector through the prison and the poorhouse. The likes of Valenod, on the other hand, are not so easily shaken. Stendhal, in fact, sums him up in this breezy paragraph:

M. Valenod was what a hundred leagues away from Paris would be known as a *bounder;* in other words a type of man who is by nature impudent and vulgar. His triumphant career, from 1815 onwards, had made such fine natural tendencies more marked. He governed Verrières, so to speak, under orders from M. de Rênal, but as he was much more active, blushed at nothing, had a finger in everyone's pie, was always on the go, writing, talking, overlooking snubs, and advancing no claims to personal importance, he had ended up by gaining equal repute with the Mayor in the eyes of the ecclesiastical authorities. M. de Valenod had, as it were, said to the grocers of the district: "Pick me out the two stupidest men amongst you"—to the lawyers: "Point me out your two greatest dunces"—to the medical officers of health: "Tell me who are your two greatest quacks." When he had collected the most shameless members of every calling, he said to them: "Now let's govern together." (Penguin, 161)

The description will do for his master as well, since M. de Rênal is represented as merely a finer alloy of the same metal—hence doomed, by the end of the tale, to make way for his more forcefully unscrupulous confederate.

In his brief exile from Vergy, following upon the arrival of an anonymous letter, Julien is given a closer glance at the rising middle class, assembled round Valenod's dinner table. Wealthy manufacturers and their ruddy-faced ladies vie with petty officials in gawking at the Rênals' tutor, spouting Latin for his dinner, while the hosts announce the price of every wine they drink. A prisoner is silenced, who, in his cell on the other side of the partition, had intoned a bawdy song. The thought that the poor wretches who went hungry to pay for the ostentatious luxury of his meal were not even permitted to sing costs Julien a tear. The heady mixture of heartlessness, wheedling, and self-importance called for to get on in this world is clearly beyond his reach.[1] And the rush of these so-called Liberal worthies to ingratiate themselves with a government that could, if it cared, rain scholarships on their children, puts the finishing touch to the portrayal of the bourgeoisie: a weak vessel indeed for the hopes of mankind stirred up by the French Revolution!

The relative gentility of M. de Rênal shines forth by contrast with the class that is soon to take over from the Squirearchy (in 1830, the July monarchy is around the corner). Yet that hard-headed, hard-hearted, egotistical vain man sums up in his person all that is contemptible and hateful in the existing order. All pomposity at home, he is a ruthlessly venal, self-serving toady in the affairs of the commune he rules, in strict obedience to Paris (and ecclesiastical) directives. Rather than lift a finger to save his childhood friend Falcoz from ruin when his paper is closed down on orders from the Congregation, he writes him "in the style of an old Roman" that the printing business ought to be turned into a State monopoly, like the sale of tobacco. "That man on his roof . . ." to whom his wife alludes is a painful reminder of the part taken by the Mayor in the repressive measures of 1816. The full measure of the man is taken, however, in the sleepless night spent in deliberating his conduct toward his wife and Julien, after the anonymous notification of his domestic misfortune.—Perhaps she is innocent after all: I am used to her, I need her.—But what if I am turned into a figure of fun, like Charmier, who is always called Bernard's Charmier, after the man who shames him?—I'll kill them both: they won't be able to laugh at me. *But the thought of blood made him fearful.*—I'll give this insolent tutor a thrashing.—Yet think of what the papers will do to me! my ancient name dragged through the mud, in the Paris press. . . .—If I don't kill my wife, and merely throw her out, she'll return to her rich aunt, whose fortune is then lost to me. . . ." Such is the great man's quandary, mercifully steered to a happier resolution by the wiles of the two conspirators, who guide him by slow stages onto the trail of Valenod, to whose disappointed love suit the "false" denunciation is laid.

Julien exchanges the relative well-being of the Rênal household for the next stage in his wavering fortunes: the Besançon seminary. The watchword here is *grime.* From the repellent aspect of the porter to the unwashed louts who are the future priests of France, from the staggeringly unkind glance of Father Pirard[2] to the vicious tactics of his enemy, Father Castanède, everything in this haunt of perverted religion smacks of moral and physical dirt. *Sale* is an adjective that comes easily to the pen of Stendhal when he writes of priests, yet Pirard himself, who is the soul of honor, and the venerable Chélan are among the few noble souls encountered in the world of the novel. True, Chélan loses his living and Pirard, actively persecuted as a Jansenist, eventually resigns his precarious rectorship of the seminary. But those are two anti-Establishment types in a Church that has sold out to the Establishment, in fact *runs* the Establishment, having baldly exchanged the saving of its soul for the gaining of the whole world. Spying, lying, vying for favor with one's superiors, abjuring all thought and all feeling, save only the official doctrine—"the party line"—masters and pupils alike wallow in moral uncleanness. Julien's inability to seem ignoble *from the heart* marks him out in spite of his best efforts as "a Martin Luther"! His trunk is searched, his mind picked clean in a final examination where his knowledge of the classics (abhorrently profane!) is ferreted out of him by a wily examiner—with a resultant ranking of 198th for Father Pirard's brilliant protégé! Greater refinement awaits him at the bishop's palace, where His Grace, bemused by the high protection evidenced by Julien's imminent removal to Paris, takes pleasure in the conversation of a seminarian well-read in the Roman poets. But even here the Vicar-general Frilair is in attendance, a timely reminder that intrigue and persecution are brewed on high with the same infernal zeal as in the noisome pit below.

The noble household of the Marquis de La Mole, in its setting of late eighteenth-century Parisian splendor, the Hôtel de La Mole, would seem to lie beyond the curse of bog-land mentality, reserved for the lower orders, shamelessly striving after money and power. Power is a birthright in these parts: it lies easily on the bony shoulders of the witty marquis, heir to the dry matter-of-fact eighteenth-century understanding of life, which sets private pleasure at the top of its scale of values—so far is he from giving in to the gloomy mean-spiritedness of his own day and age. M. de La Mole is among the half-dozen men who rule the destinies of the nation: his power, his wealth are on a scale that dwarfs the spheres in which our hero has moved so far—and he has the gifts of intellect and resolution to match his means. A tiny deity sets all this splendor at naught: *ennui* is its name.

Relentless, ferocious boredom torments this noble house. The brilliant receptions, the gilded youth, the eager toadies—none escape the iron law: no original word must be spoken, no unfamiliar thought entertained—lest it give occasion for ridicule or fall prey to censure. Fearful of being laughed at or thought unconventional, the elegant Parisians walk their appointed rounds and speak their appointed pieces, the men confined to horsemanship and physical daring, the women to flirtation and toilette. An occasional fop like the Chevalier de Beauvoisis or the Russian Prince Korasoff spices futility with a dash of good nature, but they are more than made up for by the humorless pietism of Madame de Fervaques, the marshall's widow so feverishly resolved to bury her commoner origins in fashionable devotion. Small wonder then that Julien conquers the gout-ridden marquis with his bright, sensible comments on the news of the day, his intelligent selection of articles culled even from the forbidden press. And how is the headstrong Mathilde, surrounded by her bevy of brilliant, valorous, empty-headed suitors, not to fall under the charm of this saturnine commoner, whose every glance is fired by a thought —the boldest, most original, most perilous thought of all: the overthrow of that whole iniquitous, insatiable, bloody-minded world of hers?

"Tell me what you dream of, I shall tell you who you are": such might be Stendhal's version of that oft-restated adage. Does any doubt remain, therefore, of the essential bog-land vulgarity of the exalted La Moles, when we remember that the marquise only came to life when the conversation turned to the Crusades (to which she traced her lineage), and that the marquis's own heart was set on only one thing in this whole wide world: the stool of a duchess for his daughter?

II *Prefects, and Others*

The banker François Leuwen feared only two things in life: humidity and bores. His son, to earn his right to a place in that earthly paradise, his mother's salon, was to experience more than his share of both. As a servant of a regime at odds with the working class and despised by the young (with whom his republican sympathies lay), held at arm's length moreover by "society" in the fervidly Carlist[3] garrison town of Nancy, capital of the dreary Eastern marches, Lucien Leuwen was to know tedium in its two extreme manifestations: the grotesque and the claustrophobic.

Claustrophobia soon sets in through that very army life from which a young man who grew up on the heady fare of Napoleonic victories had every right to expect the breath of fresh air promised by a manly occupation, far from the miasma of moneymaking and the race for preferment. His first glimpse of his commanding officer, Colonel Filloteau, reveals: "a man of short stature and wary eye, with great blond side-whiskers, carefully combed, spreading over his cheeks. Lucien was stupefied. 'My God!' he thought, 'this man is just a pettifogger from Lower Normandy!' " *(Green Huntsman,* 14.) His brother officers turn out to be meanly envious of his wealth, a collection of sneaks and bullies against whom his sole defense is in the cold insolence that is the invariable refuge of the Stendhalian *belle âme* when faced with the arrogance of his peers. But the embodiment of the military malaise, under a government committed to peace abroad and social repression (of the "law and order" variety) at home is the figure of the general. The general and the prefect share the responsibility for the political stability, the "good behavior" of the region they watch over jointly. While the latter personage will be heard from more at length, the former deserves some notice also. The doleful report on the state of affairs in Nancy presented by Baron Thérance to the Inspector General, Count N . . . gives us a close look at the type.

Physically, the Inspector General still had a waistline, and a few carefully tended curls between blond and grey gave a certain grace to an otherwise perfectly bald head. His face revealed a steadfast courage and a firm resolve to obey, but was, in every other respect, a total stranger to thought.

It was a face that was much less pleasing at second glance and seemed almost common at the third; there was a vague aura of duplicity about it. One could see that the Empire and its servility had passed that way.

Happy the heroes who died before 1804! (25)

Valor, denseness, and a spirit broken by surrender to a parvenu despot combine, under a government that fails to compel admiration, into something more akin to an army man[4] than a soldier. The tale of woe unfolded by the commanding general: his officers jeered in the street, shunned by society, reduced to the company of wenches in the cafés; he himself in receipt of anonymous scurrilities, having to go to bed at 8 for want of suitable entertainment—does little to restore our sense of sweep and grandeur. Held to little more than police tasks which pit them against such dire threats to society as a straggling band of undernourished strikers, Napoleon's aging generals, wistfully eyeing their useless sabers, swallow the snubs and provocations, meekly taking to their beds at an unseasonable hour.

Finding army life neither dashing (socially) nor heroic, Lucien falls back on luxury. A thoroughbred horse, first-rate appointments, royal fare dished out by a retinue of servants must do service for the absent amenities of good company and noble undertakings. The purchase of a fine horse brings him before his first prefect.

> After ten minutes, Lucien saw gravely advancing toward him, a young man about four and a half feet tall, who appeared timid and arrogant at the same time. He seemed to bear, with certain pride, an admirable head of hair so blond as to appear perfectly colorless. Extremely fine and worn too long, it was parted in a meticulously drawn line that separated its owner's head in two equal sections after the German fashion. At the sight of this little figure, which apparently walked on springs, and aimed at grace as well as majesty, Lucien's anger subsided and was followed by a mad desire to laugh. . . . "This then is one of those terrible prefects against whom the liberal papers fulminate every morning!" (40)

This grotesque personage, who embodies the civil authority of the July monarchy in Nancy—although the grocer's wife, Mme Berchu, is all the company he sees, her back-parlor his sole refuge against solitude—has but one concern: not to appear to take the slightest interest in anything. Self-importance in a dandified dwarf is perhaps much to take: the institutionalization of unbearable mediocrity could not be more slashingly symbolized.

Diminished stature, in fact, is not the privilege of the governing majority. Dr. Du Poirier, the ideologue of the reactionary opposition, is himself a hunchback.[5] The stillborn feudal pretensions of the closed little society in which allegiance is sworn to the Bohemian exile, and post-Revolutionary France and all its works consigned to simple nonexistence, are aptly represented by the crippled figure of its thinking-master. The insanely ambitious Du Poirier sees through the folly of his titled faithful but rejoices in the power to mold their thoughts, as he looks forward to a political career powered by their support. Meanwhile Mmes de Commercy, d'Hocquincourt, de Puylaurens languish in their self-imposed exile, confined to the stultifying company of their equals, in which they mirror the sterility and isolation to which, by closing their doors in their faces, they relegate the officer corps of the 27th Lancers.

His escape from that backwater, his resignation from the Army do not set Lucien free from the lispings of fools in power, reinforced at this stage by the foul play to which, as a higher civil servant, he finds himself readily exposed. His first assignment as Master of Petitions attached to the Minister of the Interior (a man profitably embroiled with the banking house of Van Peters, Leuwen & Co. on a scheme of reciprocal tip-offs and investments) is to straighten out the "Kortis affair": the shooting of a provocateur from the secret police by a sentinel he sought to disarm, while dressed as a worker, as his part of a campaign to draw a wedge between soldiers and workers. In search of his own minister, to whom he wished to report the success of his delicate negotiations, Lucien is forced to barge in on the Minister of Foreign Affairs.

"M. le Comte, my name is Lucien Leuwen, Master of Petitions. I have a thousand excuses to offer Your Excellency. But I have been looking for M. le Comte de Vaize for the last two hours on his express order. I must speak to him about an affair that is both important and urgent."

"What ... *urgent* ... affair?" said the Minister with unparalleled fatuity, straightening his tiny stature.

"By gad," thought Lucien, "I'll make you change that tone." And with perfect composure and significant emphasis he added:

"The Kortis affair, M. le Comte, the man who was wounded on the Austerlitz Bridge by a soldier he was trying to disarm."

"You may go," said the Minister, addressing his servants . . . .

"The word Kortis, sir, would have been sufficient without explanations." His tone and manner were unbelievably insolent.

"M. le Comte, I am a novice in the affairs of state," Lucien said with marked emphasis. "In my father's circle I am not accustomed to a reception such as you have given me tonight. I wanted to bring to an end as quickly as possible a situation that was both painful and improper."

"What do you mean, sir, *improper?*" said the Minister in a pinched nasal tone, lifting his head still higher, and more insolent than ever. "You had best weigh your words, sir."

"And if you add one more in that tone, M. le Comte, we will measure swords. Impertinence, sir, has never impressed me."

(Telegraph, 90—91)

Thus the impolitic Lucien, who need not fear Count Beausobre's sword (it remains prudently sheathed) but will owe to him a reputation, carefully disseminated through the salons, of Saint-Simonian thinking.

Telling off a minister is to be good practice for Lucien's further duties: as commissioner of elections in two separate districts he will find himself confronted with two further specimens of the genus *prefect,* a breed no more impressive in its provincial apprenticeship than grown to full size, at the head of a ministry.

[73]

His first prefect, M. de Riquebourg, receives him in the late evening in his cotton nightcap, and the *bonhomie* of this high official, who instructs the cook in person and chats with his barber "to keep in touch" appears not to belie that informal apparel. M. de Riquebourg has four daughters to marry off, the great landowners in his district treat directly with the Royal Court over his head, his electoral woes are many, and Lucien is almost ready to forgive him his servile bowings and scrapings in the direction of the absent Minister, when two circumstances jar him into a more realistic appraisal of the man. His "grand maneuver" to dispose of the opposition candidate, who is favored to win, is a bogus notification on election day to that great lumber merchant that some of his major clients from Nantes may default on their payments. The man's prompt removal from the polls to the town in question is thus assured, his credit badly shaken, and a perfectly sound business likely headed for bankruptcy. Such fetid machinations invite Lucien not to spare the vanity of the mealy-mouthed strategist. He tells him that his prize possession, the letters from the Minister in longhand, locked away for safekeeping in a special vault, are in fact in the handwriting of one of the secretaries:

"What! It isn't His Excellency's?" cried the Prefect, aghast. "I have some knowledge of handwriting, gentlemen!"

And as M. de Riquebourg was not thinking about his voice, it had taken on a very sharp and sarcastic tone, half-reproachful, half-threatening.

"The true Prefect tone," Lucien thought. "There is no calling like it to ruin a man's voice. Three-quarters of the rudeness of M. de Vaize comes from his having for ten years held forth alone in the drawing room of his Prefecture." (175)

Lucien promptly leaves behind this much-burdened official, passing up the chance for an intimate dinner at which only seventeen people were asked, to tackle the larger object of his mission: to block the election, in Caen, of a man of sense and character, the opposition candidate Mairobert. The Prefect, M. Boucault de Séranville, a turncoat pre-1830 Liberal, receives him coldly (his reward for letting Lucien cool his heels is to discover him deeply engrossed in those firebrand pre-1830 broadsides of his, thoughtfully collected by the opposition and bound in red covers!). Tiny (once again!) and exquisitely turned out, grimacing with resentment at the envoy from Paris, this prefect clearly is not about to extend a finger to further a mission which reflects adversely on his quite incompetent stewardship. To cable the bad news that Mairobert is a "shoo-in," Lucien must well-nigh come to blows with the incensed dandy.

M. de Séranville was plainly annoyed. He read over Lucien's credentials several times and, on the whole, behaved exactly like his employee at the cable office. . . . Exasperated at having lost three-quarters of an hour already, Lucien said finally:

"At least, sir, deign to give me a clear, straightforward answer."

"I endeavor, sir, always to make myself clear."

"Then, sir, are you or are you not willing to have my dispatch sent?"

"It seems to me, sir, that I might see that dispatch. . . ."

"You avoid, sir, that clarity which you just led me to expect, after three-quarters of an hour already wasted."

"Your objection, sir, might, it seems to me, be couched in a tone rather more . . ."

Lucien interrupted the Prefect, who was by now pale with rage:

"I cannot admit further quibbling. It is getting late. To defer your answer is to give it in the negative without daring to admit as much."

"Daring, sir!"

"Will you or will you not allow my dispatch to go through?"

"Very well, sir! For the moment I am still the Prefect of Calvados and my answer is: *No."*

This *no* was spoken with all the fury of an outraged martinet.

"Sir," replied Lucien, "I shall have the honor of making my request in writing. I trust that you will dare to make your reply in writing as well, and I shall immediately send a courier to the Minister."

"A courier! A courier! You will have neither horses, nor courier, nor passport. Are you aware, sir, that at the——Bridge there is an order signed by me to let no one through without a passport, and a passport bearing a certain distinguishing mark?"

"Very well, Monsieur le Préfet!" and Lucien paused deliberately between each word, "from the moment you refuse to obey the instructions of the Minister of the Interior, there is no longer any government. I have orders for General Fari, and I shall ask him to arrest you."

"Arrest *me,* damn you!"

And the little Prefect hurled himself at Lucien who, picking up a chair, warded him off.

"With such behavior, sir, you will first be well thrashed and then arrested. Perhaps that will satisfy you." (199–200)

Surely a richly satisfying way to lose an election! It scarcely comes as a surprise, after such a dose of bitter medicine, that the noble pigmy, by withdrawing the government's *own* electors, manages to spike the right-wing coalition Lucien had bravely forged with the Minister's gold: Mairobert is safe.

Lucien's ultimate trial by pretentious mediocrity comes in the course of the courtship instituted by his father as a remedy for the twin evils of lovesickness and supposed Saint-Simonian leanings. Madame Grandet is that authentic vulgarian, whose cold heart lays an empty claim to virtue, whose prosy mind aspires to a fashionable elevation. *That beautiful body,* in Lucien's phrase, *plays host to the soul of a chambermaid.* But the therapeutic boredom of his courtship is occasionally enlivened by a scene in which the reigning idol is, with some cruelty, revealed to walk on feet of clay:

That evening a painfully thin young German scholar, with a mass of blond hair parted in the middle, had been presented to Madame Grandet. She was talking to him about all the learned discoveries made by Germans: Homer had perhaps written only one of the famous "Homeric hymns" whose masterly treatment, the fruit of chance, is so admired by pedants. Madame Grandet spoke very well of the Alexandrian School. A large group had gathered around her. The subject of Christian antiquities was brought up and Madame Grandet immediately looked serious and gave the corners of her mouth a downward twist.

Then, of all things, what did this newly presented German do, but attack the Catholic mass to a bourgeois woman of the court of Louis-Philippe? These Germans are the very kings of tactlessness!

"The Mass in the Fifth Century," he explained, "was nothing but a social gathering at which bread was broken in memory of Jesus Christ. It was a sort of tea party for the faithful. . . ."

"Good God! Where ever did you find all that, my dear sir?" cried Madame Grandet, horrified. "In some of your German authors, most likely, although they are usually so sympathetic to sublime and mystical ideas, and for that very reason are cherished by all right-thinking people. . . ."

"No, Madam. The French too have very great scholars," replied the young German dialectician. . . . "But as French literature, Madam, is so rich and the French have so many treasures, they are like people with enormous wealth, ignorant of the treasures they possess. This whole authentic story of the Mass I found in old Father Mabillon. . . ."

Madame Grandet was exceedingly vexed.

"How wonderful Madame de Staël would have been in a moment like this," she thought, "surrounded by such a large attentive audience! I see at least thirty people listening to us and here I am, incapable of finding a word in reply, and it is too late to become indignant!"   (130—32)

Lucien read his duty in her distracted glance and leapt into the breach: but alas! our German was proof against persiflage. He had the facts, and he stuck to them.

The inhabitants of the flatlands are thus often recognizable by the airs with which they grace their incurable insignificance. Like the frog of La Fontaine's fable, they swell up their small size with desperate endeavor. But beauty itself, bereft of kindness and simplicity, is not proof against the inevitable deflation. Witness the fate of that same Madame Grandet, who sells herself to Lucien for a cabinet post for her husband, only to fall in love with the youth after he learns of the transaction: a stony heart, a grubby mind are not passports to felicity in the novels of Stendhal!

III   *A Father and a Court*

While the carpenter Sorel seems to combine the fearfulness attached to the joint memory of aunt Séraphie and the *abbé* Raillane, and the banker Leuwen reflects the admiration mingled with affection felt for Dr. Henri Gagnon, the perhaps unjust aversion Chérubin Beyle managed to stir in his son's breast is patently encased in the pale swollen features of the hateful Marchese del Dongo, ostensibly the father of Fabrizio. His fear of the French invaders equals his hatred for the reign of sheer delight they inaugurate, the overdue explosion of long pent-up high spirits in the oppressed people of Milan. Leaving his beautiful young wife to the tender mercies of those fiends, the Marchese locks himself up in the fortified castle of Grianta: "surrounded by some twenty-five or thirty retainers whom he supposed to be devoted to his person, presumably because he never opened his mouth except to curse them. (Anchor, 15). His generosity is a match for his gallantry. He openly boasts of not sending a penny to his sister Countess Pietranera, who starves in France with her Piedmontese general. His elder son Ascanio, a faithful reflection of so worthy a father, denounces Fabrizio to the Austrian police on his return from Waterloo, in hopes of securing for him a lifetime in chains in the depths of some fortress dungeon. Under the French-backed rule of Prince Eugene the loyal Marchese earns another star from his rightful sovereign by his inaccurate but pleasing weekly dispatches to the court in Vienna, coded in greatest secrecy with the help of Ascanio:

it was the fifth to adorn his Chamberlain's coat. As a matter of fact, he suffered from the chagrin of not daring to sport this garment outside his study; but he never allowed himself to dictate a despatch without first putting on the gold-laced coat, studded with all his orders. He would have felt himself to be wanting in respect had he acted otherwise.   (21)

The spirit of reaction, the hatred for new ideas (for *ideas*, in fact) wears an unflattering expression in a country where the old regime is that of a foreign occupation, and the prerogative of high birth the right to fawn (for the sake of privilege) upon an absent ruler.

The court of Parma, on the other hand, which mirrors the other twin evils of Italian political life—its splintered state and the despotism of divine right princelings—combines the two requisites of bog-land surreality:

dead-earnest self-importance and pinhead-sized constriction. The presence
in that court, in the unlikely role of prime minister, of that quiet ironist
Mosca and his dazzlingly spirited mistress Gina, now Duchessa Sanseverina-Taxis, insures that stuffiness will not go unrecognized, nor be allowed
to rule unchallenged by at least a breath of fresh air. The sovereign is a
man who feels constrained to look under all palace beds at night for fear
of Liberal conspirators (this is the task that Mosca has had the charity and
the wit to take over from him, unsmiling). His minister of justice is an
adroit, unscrupulous blackguard with only one passion:

he loved to converse with eminent personages and to please them by
buffooneries. It mattered little to him whether the powerful personage
laughed at what he said or at his person, or uttered revolting pleasantries at
the expense of Signora Rassi.... Sometimes the Prince, at a loss how
further to insult the dignity of this Chief Justice, would actually kick him;
if the kicks hurt him he would begin to cry. (261)

The more or less official opposition party is headed by Contessa Raversi, a
tireless intriguer, and General Fabio Conti, a mindless martinet (Fabrizio's
future jailer). To complete the picture there is the timid, learned,
commoner-born Archbishop Landriani, infinitely respectful of titled
heads.[6]

Anxious boredom is the curse of power when it is both absolute and
trifling in its range. The games the Duchessa must play—to make her salon
the one place where the Prince is never dull is the backbone of her
policy—and the uglier games the Prince himself will play to ward off that
yawning monster (such as sending Mosca an anonymous letter denouncing
Gina's love for her nephew, to be delivered moments before a summons to
appear before his Sovereign) speak volumes on that topic. In fact, the
whole of political life in the diminutive kingdom soon revolves around this
weighty proposition: how is the Prince to get even with the Duchessa for
holding him at arm's length, without exposing himself to her swift removal
to Naples, where she can laugh at him with full impunity and leave him, by
the same token, a prey to ennui? The king's gambit is the blowing up of
the scuffle with Giletti into an affair of state. Fabrizio goes into exile. The
Duchessa requests an audience.

the Prince . . . was not at all surprised, still less annoyed by this request
for an audience. "We shall see tears flowing from fine eyes," he said to
himself, rubbing his hands. . . . "Ask the Signora Duchessa to wait for a
quarter of an hour." The General Aide-de-Camp made his half turn, like a
soldier on parade. . . . This quarter of an hour was exquisite for the Prince;
he walked up and down with a firm and steady pace; he *reigned.* (249–50)

But his triumph is short-lived, as the tearful woman he looked forward to impressing appears in travel habit, gay and pretty as never before. His discomposure is dramatic.

> The Duchessa spoke quite slowly so as to give herself time to enjoy the spectacle of the Prince's face; it was delicious, by reason of the profound astonishment and of the traces of the grand manner which the position of his arms and head still betrayed. The Prince sat as though struck by a thunderbolt; in a shrill and troubled little voice he exclaimed from time to time, barely articulating the words: *"What's that! What's that!"* (250-51)

The news of her departure for Naples quite dashes his hopes for a grand scene, after the manner of Louis XIV. Her haughty recital of her grievances: "I am leaving the States of Your Serene Highness for ever, so as never to hear the names of the Fiscal Rassi and of the other infamous assassins who have condemned my nephew and so many others to death," leaves him torn between anger and admiration ("with a little policy it might not be impossible to make her my mistress").

> "And what would one have to do to make the Signora not leave us?"
> "Something of which you are not capable," replied the Duchessa in an accent of the most bitter irony and the most unconcealed contempt.
> The Prince was beside himself, but his professional training as an Absolute Sovereign gave him the strength to overcome his first impulse. "I must have this woman," he said to himself; "so much I owe to myself, then she must be made to die of shame. . . ." But, mad with rage and hatred as he was at this moment, where was he to find an answer that would at once satisfy the requirements of what he owed to himself and induce the Duchessa not to abandon his court immediately. . . . Presently he heard a tap at (the) door.
> "Who is the creature," he cried, shouting with the full force of his lungs, "who is the creature who comes here to thrust his fatuous presence upon me?" Poor General Fontana shewed a pallid face of complete discomfiture, and it was with the air of a man in his last agony that he stammered these inarticulate words: "His Excellency the Conte Mosca solicits the honour of being introduced."
> "Let him come in," said, or rather shouted the Prince. . . .   (253)

The Conte's own dismay—for he is not privy to Gina's plan and shares in the general contempt showered by her upon the court of Parma—is a balm for the Prince's humiliation. Swallowing his pride he accepts to write a letter to the Duchessa promising not to sign the sentence against Fabrizio when it is laid before him, "and that these unjust proceedings shall have no consequences for the future" (256). Alas, the Conte omits this last, most galling phrase from the text of the letter, leaving the door open for the twelve years' confinement to which Fabrizio is eventually sentenced. For the Opposition's turn to act comes next, and Contessa Raversi, jealous of the Duchessa's influence and good looks, traps Fabrizio by the use of a forged note in Gina's hand: he is dragged back in chains, and locked up in the Farnese tower. But in this contest of wiles the last word has not been spoken. The unthinkable escape from the unassailable tower, engineered by her with Clelia's complicity is accompanied by the flooding of the streets of Parma from the reservoir of Gina's castle in Sacca, where fireworks are triumphantly displayed. Ferrante Palla, the revolutionary poet in love with the spirited Duchessa, finds means to send the Prince to his untimely death, with the compliments of one who does not choose to be victimized with impunity.

In the attempted revolution the Conte holds the mob at bay. The Crown Prince rules in his father's stead, the Duchessa is the new Grand Mistress of the Dowager Princess's household, and the game is played under new rules, to suit the new cast of characters. The Prince is earnest, learned, and weak; his mother, fearful of being relegated to oblivion, is painfully dependent on the helpful ingenuity of the Grand Mistress of her household (her characteristic advice: see to it that yours is the only salon where he enjoys himself!).

Bullying her weak sovereign and turning his head by turns, the Duchessa manages to have Fabrizio retried, but the enraged Fabio Conti has no intention of releasing his prisoner alive, after enduring the affront of a successful escape from the fortress entrusted to his care. To save her nephew from the plot to poison him Gina is forced to grant the Prince her ultimate favors. She leaves for Naples and marries the Conte, while the coadjutor, later Archbishop del Dongo, by a series of fiery sermons creates such a stir in Parma that the Marchesa Crescenzi herself must needs attend one, to fall once more under his spell.

Though the *happy few* stay clear of the deadly waters reserved for those who breathe only cowardice, envy, and selfishness, even they must pay the price of the deplorable company that, like the rest of us in this world, they are required to keep.

Clelia married off to Crescenzi, Fabrizio ending up a monk, Gina taken against her will, Mosca back in harness at the end give witness to the kind of victory with which the bog of this world can be credited. Their solace and ours is that they do not succumb.

CHAPTER 4

Euclid

> Cet heureux XVIIIe siècle où il n'y avait
> rien à haïr.

IN *Le Rose et le vert* (1837) the German heroine Mina de Wanghen runs into an honest and sagacious man in the whirlwind of Paris frivolity: her literature master M. Hiéky.[1] He marvels at her rare understanding of La Bruyère (which seems to him scarcely compatible with her pleasure in the sparrows picking at crumbs on the balcony) and proceeds to elaborate, in his comments on that master:

"In this city of Paris, which had five hundred thousand inhabitants in Napoleon's day and today numbers eleven hundred thousand, all sorts of people are to be found, the best and the worst. Cut a hole through the wall of the salon in one house and you'll find on the same floor, in the corresponding room on the other side of the wall, people of character perfectly antithetical to that of the people gathered in the first salon."

. . . .

—But tell us, sir, if such and such a salon holds all that is most crude, most vulgar, most disgusting in the world, isn't that probability enough to cause a like population to be found in the next salon?

—Either you have stumbled, Mademoiselle, or you have not deigned to give this matter all your attention: these people who are quite crude, vulgar, etc., etc., were indeed remarkable through some superiority.

—Bravo, Professor, Madame Wanghen cried out, you're getting the better of my daughter.

—Mother is right, sir, said Mina. Those people had the superiority of wealth. . . . As you're kindly disposed toward me, sir, do explain to me the variety of the Paris salons.

—To one who has eyes to see, nothing is so much alike as the passions, or rather the one passion, that moves those Parisian hearts: the *wish to appear* just a bit more than what you are. The best company is distinguished by the fact that, while they still want to *appear,* it is no more than what in fact they are. *(Romans,* ll, 1104-05)

The apparent variety (some want to appear rich, others play at seeming poor) is explicable by the workings of a single principle. The striving for rigor, lucidity, and a kind of smiling matter-of-factness equally free either of bitterness or of illusion is familiar to the reader of Stendhal, as is the fact that the truth is spoken, in the dry tones of one who deals with facts and figures, by an honest, unassuming, impecunious man, who teaches for a living. The only quirk is that, in this one case, he is not a teacher of mathematics.

I *La Gaya Scienza*

Mathematics, we know, paved young Beyle's way out of small-town asphyxiation. His youthful proficiency appears to have had a twofold origin: the encounter (chronicled in *Henry Brulard)* with a first-rate teacher—the geometer Louis-Gabriel Gros—with all the excitement of intellectual awakening which knowledge rousingly imparted brings in its wake. And then (but which came first?) the touchingly simple conviction which caused him to write: "I loved, and still love, mathematics for its own sake, as incompatible with *vagueness* and *hypocrisy,* my two pet aversions" *(01,* 96).

Facts do not lie, they do not wheedle, they are possessed of no ulterior motives, they *are* what they *seem.* A curious religion for a man destined to probe so deeply the notoriously elusive terrain of human motivation, but a first-rate antidote to that *enthusiasm* so dreaded by the eighteenth-century mind, a large dose of which was to mix felicitously with a "mathematical" bias to produce the mind of Stendhal. To see things for what they are, while at the same time caring only for what might be, for the Ideal, is a richly contradictory mode of perception. "My character," as he wrote in his journal (October 31, 1823), "strains painfully to submit to the maxims of the mind to which it was harnessed by chance!"

Mathematicians, in consequence, are gaily strewn throughout the novels, as pointed reminders of the flaccid or overblown character of the generalized human landscape, itself better adapted than wiser heads to 1830 conditions and more in keeping with 1830 expectations. Lucien Leuwen is a refugee from the Ecole Polytechnique:[2] so is Octave de Malivert, in *Armance;* and so Fédor de Miossens, the young duke with whom Lamiel first elopes. Priore Blanès, Fabrizio's intellectual mentor, combines the duties of a country priest with the concerns of a mad scientist, scanning the heavens all night with a pasteboard telescope, deep in the study of the course of the planets and their omen-laden conjunctions.

Fabrizio adored him: to gratify him he sometimes spent whole evenings in doing enormous sums of addition and multiplication. Then he would go up to the belfry: this was a great favour and one that Priore Blanès had never granted to anyone; but he liked this boy for his simplicity. "If you do not turn out a hypocrite," he would say to him, "you will perhaps be a man." (Anchor, 24)

Astrology, to be sure, is not an exact science (supposing it were, thinks Fabrizio in a moment of doubt, "like three-quarters of the sciences that are not mathematical, a collection of enthusiastic simpletons and adroit hypocrites paid by the masters they serve"? 163)—it is, for Fabrizio, a *religion,* blithely absorbed in childhood, hence steeped in the felicity of moving associations. Which may be no more than to say that it is an *Italian* science, giving to that nation the peculiarly Stendhalian dream-value of homeland of the emotions, *patrie du cœur.*

Julien too was brought up by a scientist of sorts, the retired Napoleonic surgeon-major. His scientific training shows not so much in (quite nonexistent) medical information as in the ascetic objectivity with which he draws the lesson from a series of unjust fines levied by an otherwise fair-minded judge, bowing to the power of the local clergy in Verrières: to rise in the world he must forego the dreamed-of cavalryman's boots, and aim for the hateful black cassock. Committing the Latin New Testament to memory *cold,* without the slightest interest in the "message" of the text, with its freight of imperatives that give such ample room for emotional playacting, is another such feat of scientific detachment. The words ripple off his brain smoothly, leaving it unaffected save for the care that they be rendered letter perfect. Rigor and accuracy provide the mask behind which the thoughts are free, while fools and knaves are left to their tricks of compunction and awe, taking in no one but themselves.

In the end Julien himself pays the price of hypocrisy, albeit in his case the outer garment borrowed from a foe whose onslaught he could not otherwise survive. When Valenod, now a baron, calls on the Marquis de La Mole in his capacity as the new mayor of Verrières, Julien is ordered to receive him well. Masking his distaste in a show of Machiavellian solidarity, Julien requests the newly-vacated poorhouse directorship for his father, and the lottery bureau for M. Chollin, whose abject and illiterate petition, picked up on the church floor after the King's visit to Verrières, had given him a moment's entertainment. The patronage is cheerfully granted, when Julien learns to his grief that a deputation from the department "had asked for this post for M. Gros, the celebrated mathematician. This noble-hearted man had an income of only fourteen hundred francs, and had been lending six hundred francs every year to the late holder of the post, to help him bring up his family" (Penguin, 292). The game of power requires the coolest head, for it soon fogs the clearest lenses.

Unvarnished home truths find their way to the ear of restless young Leuwen, squirming on his bed of ease. His cousin Ernest Dévelroy, slated for the Institute of Moral Sciences, pours cold water on his gilded woes: give over these unassuming airs, take a stand, be grave, look the part of a man of substance if you want to be taken seriously—or someday the world will take its revenge on you for not conforming to its ways, and you'll have to go in for horse races to drown your sorrows. When Colonel Filloteau's tired wheelhorse appearance and unelevated concerns get him down Dévelroy upbraids him:

"What do you mean by making such a face? You look as though someone had given you some rotten *pâté de Strasbourg*. Do you or don't you want to amount to something in this world?"

"My God, what riffraff!"

"This lieutenant-colonel is worth a hundred of you. He is a peasant who, by making good use of his sword for anyone who paid him, bagged those epaulets with bullion fringe."

"But he's so coarse, so disgusting! . . ."

"All the more credit to him! it was by disgusting his superiors, if they were worth more than he, that he forced them to favor the advancement he enjoys today. And you, my worthy republican, have you ever earned a penny in your life? . . . Aren't you ashamed, at your age, not to be able to earn so much as the price of a cigar?"

(Green Huntsman, 14-5)

And it is to him that we owe that biting and far from inaccurate characterization of Lucien as a lover, which the latter in the first flush of his "conquest" of Madame Grandet makes bold to refute at last:

For once Ernest was wrong when he predicted that never in my life would I win a respectable woman without being in love with her, in other words, that I could only succeed through pity and tears—what that miserable chemist calls the *watery way*.

(Telegraph, 335)

But the burden of scientific rigor and detachment in the face of adversity is taken up by Lucien's former classmate, also expelled from Polytechnique on political grounds, the mordant, penniless, austere Coffe, who journeys with him on his electoral mission. When mud is quite literally slung at the two envoys by an enraged mob, apprized of their capacity as government agents, the habitually silent Coffe takes his heartsick travel companion in hand (there's a man who "actually believed he could combine the advantages of the Ministry with the delicate susceptibilities of a man of honor"! *Tel.,* 158), dousing him with the icy waters of an unadorned view of their plight:

"You are not thick-skinned enough not to feel the public's scorn. But one gets used to it. All you have to do is to transfer your vanity elsewhere. Look at M. de Talleyrand. As in the case of that celebrated man—when scorn gets too commonplace it's only fools that bother giving voice to it. Thus the fools among us spoil everything, even scorn."

"That's strange consolation you offer me," retorted Lucien somewhat curtly.

"The only kind for you, it seems to me. When one undertakes the thankless task of consoling a brave man, one must first of all speak the truth. I am a surgeon, cruel only in appearance. I probe the wound deeply, but in order to cure it.

(160)

Later on Lucien is scoffed at by a cudgel-bearing bully, quite unintimidated by the Master of Petitions' challenge to a duel. Coffe, remembering how he himself had been roughed up by police *provocateurs,* chaffs him about it. Lucien speaks bullets and pistols, and Coffe retorts:

"You can kill this disguised gendarme with impunity. He has orders not to lose his temper. Yet, perhaps at Montmirail or Waterloo, he was a brave soldier. Today we're all in the same regiment," Coffe added with a bitter laugh. "Let's not fight."

"You are cruel," said Lucien.

"I speak the truth when I am asked, take it or leave it."

Tears filled Lucien's eyes.

The carriage was now allowed to enter the city. On reaching the inn, Lucien seized Coffe's hand:

"I am a child," he said.

"Not at all, you are simply one of the privileged class of this age, as the preachers say, and you have never had disagreeable work to do."

(185-86)

A Sancho Panza filled with the authority of his unblinking honesty and straight thinking watches over this youthfully irritable Quixote.

Chemists and mathematicians do not exhaust the striving for a kind of unillusioned objectivity in which Stendhal sought refuge from the portentous and the bogus. To "derousseau-ize" himself is a cure his journal prescribes in the form of a reading of Tacitus and Destutt de Tracy (May 23, 1804). In an age of stylistic inflation highlighted by Chateaubriand's sonorous flights and Madame de Staël's grandiloquent poses, Stendhal opts for dryness. The sole merit he wishes to claim for himself is "that I write what I think." *(OI, Journal,* 1137) Immortal writings, to his way of thinking, are penned by men who give little thought to style. "I imagine that the author wrote while carried away by his own thoughts *per sfogarsi* [to give free flow] " he writes in his journal (March 4, 1818). Although his celebrated boast to Balzac, that he read over a few pages of the civil code every morning while working on the *Charterhouse of Parma,* need not be taken literally (it is rather a typical Stendhalian quip, with which to ward off the stylistic advice of a man who writes, without blushing, *it snows in my heart*[3]), it reflects the trend of his stylistic preoccupations. Long before he was to be a writer, he had in his journal (October 12, 1808) defined the manner he was one day to make his own: "My style will find its own character in poking fun at everyone; it will be accurate *(juste);* and it won't induce sleep."

The fear of all sentimental overstatement (what the French call, untranslatably, *pudeur)* happily mingled, in Stendhal, with the joyful awareness sounded by the following line in *The Memoirs of an Egotist* (1832): "It is my good fortune to go on being taken in by women just as at the age of twenty-five." *(01,* 1479) Rousseau could not be altogether dislodged, and Stendhal's writing reflects the tenderness of his heart through the hard prism of the mind: Rousseau, as it were, reviewed by Voltaire. Hence the kind of juxtaposition exemplified in the following passage, taken from Julien's stint as assistant decorator of the cathedral ruled over by Father Chas-Bernard:

The deeply sonorous tones of this bell should not have awakened anything in Julien but the thought of twenty men working for fifty centimes apiece, aided, perhaps, by fifteen or twenty pious worshippers. He should have thought of the wear and tear on the bell-ropes and the wooden framework, of the risk to the bell itself which comes tumbling down every two hundred years. He should have reflected on some way of reducing the wages of these bell-ringers or of paying them by means of some indulgence or grace drawn from the rich resources of the Church, yet making her purse no leaner.

Instead of such sage reflections, Julien's spirit, borne upwards on the rich, bass tones of the bell, was wandering through worlds upon worlds of the imagination.

(Penguin, 206-7)

In the original, two phrases *("Les sons si graves de cette cloche . . ."* and *"l'âme de Julien, exaltée par ces sons si mâles et si pleins, errait dans les espaces imaginaires")* sum up the poetry of church bells that had inspired in Chateaubriand some of his most celebrated cadences. They evoke, but do not spell out, the music that breaks down Julien's habitual self-possession and sends his soul soaring aloft. The three adjectives *grave, mâles, pleins* strike the note in the bass register expressive of the sound of brass, with the suggestion of martial resolve and calm composure—the very hymn of Julien's deeper nature! And yet, for all its restraint this rare lyrical flight, in which the author's own music-loving soul peeps through,[4] is severely encased in a paragraph of mock-censure—as worthy of Voltaire's pen as the rest is of Rousseau's—in which the, ironies bounce off one another in a joyful-sardonic cascade: the dreary practical mind with its sordid (fifty centimes apiece) and farfetched (every two hundred years) imaginings, busily chipping away at the workingman's livelihood, to melt it down ultimately to the fool's gold that costs the Church nothing: indulgences! Shades of (unknown) Marx, (unborn) Lewis Carroll crowding in on Martin Luther. . . .

The celebrated "description" of the battle of Waterloo in the *Charterhouse* ("I abhor factual description. The bother of having to go through with it stops me from writing novels" *OI, Egotist,* 1420) must be set side by side with Hugo's full-dress treatment in *Les Misérables,* complete with heroic charge and cosmic rumbles, to be fully savored. Fabrizio in earnest conversation with the *cantinière,* his teacher in matters of battlefield etiquette; his wanderings through the strangely quiet landscape right up to where Marshal Ney is standing; the sight of little black lumps of soil flying off three or four feet in the air to mark the line of fire; Fabrizio lifted off his horse to let a general be remounted; Fabrizio wounded, at last, by a saber-slash from a French hussar whose flight he impeded: heroism is stripped by Stendhal of all heroics. The unvarnished truth reveals the whole spectrum of battlefield behavior, bathed in the aura of professional matter-of-factness. Fabrizio's exalted notions, a mixture of youthfulness and Tasso, give way to the practical side of his Italian character with the loss of his own blood. Still he nobly (though uselessly) stands his ground against the hulking hussar—but he is left with the question: "what had he seen, was it a battle; and if so, was that battle Waterloo?" (Anchor, 82).

Was it a battle? Am I capable of love? Am I a coward? Am I a monster? Such self-probings echo throughout the novels and even the autobiographical memoirs, giving witness to the essentially "open" character of Stendhal's account of reality, which is the very secret, the *Euclidean* secret as it were, of the life he could breathe into his writings. The unwillingness to state more than can be known, taken together with the will to set down an unadorned account of what can be ascertained, gives his prose that endearing mixture of rigor and tentativeness that has the ring of truth. "Know thyself" is the inescapable command for the creatures of an imagination steeped in the heady dreams of the Ideologue school of psychology: the helpless floundering to which the command gives occasion, in the breast of the deeply bemused hero, pays full homage to a finitude the Ideologues seemed to have left perilously out of their reckoning.

Next to Fabrizio's Waterloo, Julien's two bedroom scenes, in *The Red and the Black,* give us our clearest glimpse of this method of gentle debunking, whereby a truth of human experience is restored to its authentic dimensions, with no loss but of false pride and overblown expectations. Sex, quite apart from the fact that the conventions of the day rule out all but the most veiled allusion to the realities it betokens, is next to war the most hallowed repository of flattering fictions. Not even the anatomic explicitness of Sade or the alcove tussles in Laclos escape the toils of mythologization. Whether the experience is set down as sublimity veiled in gauze, or recorded as a lurid skewering of maidenheads by priapic monks, it has little in common with the garden variety experience of everyday mankind. Stendhal's originality can therefore be viewed as twofold: he dares to represent matters that go on behind the closed bedroom door, and he does so with faithful regard for unheroic, unecstatic probability. Julien strides into Mme de Rênal's bedroom at two o'clock in the morning; but far from sweeping her off her feet, he collapses ignominiously before her indignant gaze, broken and in tears from the most cruel exertion of his young life: obedience to a summons to duty which, as we have seen,[5] Beyle himself had earlier failed to obey. Tears effected what a most implausible Don Juan stance, in a totally inexperienced 18-year-old, could scarcely have achieved: the bodily surrender of a self-respecting woman, in love for the first time in her own (not much older) life. Nor did lovemaking by itself bring the happiness that was to come only when trust and emotional surrender could take the place, in Julien's heart, of his soldierly conqueror stance.

Good heavens! Is being happy, is being loved no more than that? were Julien's first thoughts when he got back to his room. He was in that state of amazement and tumultuous agitation into which man's spirit sinks on obtaining what he has so long desired. The heart, grown used to desiring, finds nothing more to desire, but has as yet no memories. Like a soldier returning from parade Julien was busily absorbed in reviewing every detail of his conduct. Have I been wanting in anything I owe to myself? Have I played my part well?

And what a part! That of a man accustomed to success in his dealings with women.

(Penguin, 104)

The scene in Mathilde's bedroom is drawn out in greater detail, reflecting the interminable length of a night spent in the bedroom of a young woman, herself totally inexperienced, by a young man scarcely more knowledgeable, for whom this proud heiress is still something of a stranger. The outpouring of class and personal pride with which Mathilde's midnight summons had at first been greeted was soon to give way to gloomy misgivings and premonitions of foul play. By the time Julien makes his way up the gardener's ladder to the lighted window of his would-be mistress his mind reels with thoughts of ambush, his pockets bulge with pistols. Yet once his fears are swept away, the main emotion shared by Mathilde and Julien is that of acute embarrassment. What does one talk about at such a moment? The pistols are a conversational godsend, and they both seize on it eagerly, following it up with the disposal of the ladder and the problem of his exit (at which point they lapse into a kind of baby talk).

Mathilde was forcing herself to adopt an intimate tone; she was evidently more attentive to this unfamiliar way of addressing him than to what she was actually saying. Such endearments, utterly bare of any note of tenderness, gave Julien no pleasure after the first moment. He was amazed at his lack of happiness; finally, in order to feel it, he appealed to reason. He saw himself esteemed by this very proud girl, who never bestowed unrestricted praise, and, with the help of this argument, he attained to a happiness based on self-esteem.   (351)

Mathilde's disappointment more than matches his own. Torn between regret at her rashness, the humiliation of her position, the sufferings of shyness and wounded modesty, she finds that

She had not for a moment anticipated the dreadful state in which she now found herself.

I must speak to him, though, she finally said to herself. That's an ordinary convention, one does speak to one's lover. And then, to carry out this duty, and with a tenderness far more evident in the words she used than in the tone of her voice, she told him of the various decisions to which she had come with regard to him in the course of the last few days.

She had decided that if he ventured to come to her room with the aid of the gardener's ladder, as she had told him to do, she would be wholly his. Yet never had things so tender been said in a colder and more formal tone. It was enough to make one hate the very idea of love.   (352)

At last, "after long wavering," Mathilde and Julien taste the mingled joys of physical love. "To tell the truth, their transports were somewhat forced. Passionate love was still more of a model they were imitating than the real thing." The case could not be better stated, nor the agony of translating the mere cerebration of an *amour de tête* into the gestures of physical passion more incisively portrayed. Today's chroniclers of the sexual act in all its monotonous glory bypass the question by reducing the scope of the protagonists' emotions, which seem anchored pretty firmly to the erogenous zones (as in Updike's *Couples,* for instance). This does leave out of their reckoning that whole daylight self, which must somehow be gotten past the bedroom doors, alongside the stirring priapus.[6] Stendhal, for whom love was all, did not let that passionate conviction deter him from setting down the facts of life without shame or undue gloating. His lovers, like most of us, start out by being inept—and, like most of us, get over it. Sex neither hallows nor does it get the better of them. Their preoccupations mostly take them elsewhere (conquest, adoration, bliss), but sooner or later love, good fortune or mere chance does clear that hurdle for them, bringing them that much closer to their sole true object: the ecstasy of two souls commingled into one.

II *Fathers and Sons*

Perhaps the ultimate embodiment of Stendhal's Euclidean ideal is to be found in the figures of the Benevolent Fathers, steeped each in his own fashion in an eighteenth-century version of the *Realpolitik* to which a later age affixed a grimmer face. Lucien Leuwen, as we have seen, is unique among Stendhal's heroes in having for a father a man whose enlightened love for his son, though clearly a reflection of his passionate concern for his wife, has every chance, under the pen of a man whose own father was his *bête noire,* to correspond to what Freud so endearingly calls *simple wish fulfillment.* Julien's father is hard and mean, Fabrizio's putative parent a toad. Neither youth is altogether dispossessed, however. Their author obligingly calls on art where nature fails, forging a series of bonds out of the workings of choice and chance, to take the place of the missing paternal affection. The surgeon-major, Father Chélan, Father Pirard keep the child's heart and mind alive, before their charge is handed over to the all-powerful Marquis de La Mole, who will make of him his trusted companion. Priore Blanès does as much for Fabrizio, until the time comes when the Prime Minister of Parma, Conte Mosca, takes him under his wing. M. de La Mole, François Leuwen, Conte Mosca each represent a flowering of power and affection that make of them idealized fathers, who teach mastery of the world by example, while tactfully dispensing the means to emulate their eminence.

M. de La Mole's is the most spectacular such intervention in a young man's destiny. Armed with the wealth, the power, the prestige of a great name allied to vast estates, operating from the remote and brilliant center of French political life in Paris, the marquis balks the might of the Church itself, and snatches Julien from the hell of the Besançon seminary, to raise him at a stroke of the pen to a lofty station at that great man's side, in the Hôtel de La Mole. The post of private secretary to a man who makes or breaks a cabinet is a steep rise for the lately persecuted seminarian, a geometric progression to the arithmetic one that took him from the cuffs and blows of the sawmill to the position of Latin tutor in the Rênal household. But more significant, to one of Julien's temper, than the range of his protector's power is the *quality* that greatness on such a scale brings along with it. Typically, Stendhal makes the shift palpable, from the scope of a provincial worthy like Rênal to that of a *grand seigneur* in Paris, by having Julien step on the marquis' heel from force of habit, as the latter fails to rush ahead of him as did his former master, to beat him to the door. Exquisite manners (which extend to one's subordinates), the eagle glance of a man used to dealing with vast matters, a healthy regard for the importance of pleasure[7] mark La Mole out for an aristocrat whose formative years had been spent in the final glow of the *ancien régime*, the setting of the much vaunted but now extinct *douceur de vivre*.

The inner sense of his own greatness, or rather the constant attention to *what he owes it to himself* to do or not to do as a sign of his greatness, makes Julien immune to the heady joys of familiarity with the rulers of the earth. This noble disdain for what others seek at the cost of a thousand slights serves him well in the La Mole household. Taken together with his obvious ability, his determination to rise superior to his own short-comings,[8] his aptitude to rise, in private, above the stock phrases and conventional attitudes *de rigueur* in the public apartments, it gains him the marquis's trust and affection, even before it turns the head of his strong-willed daughter. Those two, Julien and the marquis, recognize each other across the chasm of class differences for men of the same stamp, fit to rule over others through a common contempt for the ready-made thoughts and beliefs which keep others *in their places.* Class loyalty in fact, though it keeps them apart, is a further proof of their kinship. Julien's worship of the Revolution is his version of the mystique that makes of the Crusades the only subject that wrings heartfelt seriousness from La Mole. Stendhal even goes so far as to depict the plot to foster an English-backed allied invasion of France to forestall the rebellion of the middle and lower classes, in which La Mole is linked with the highest lay and ecclesiastical personages of the (Restoration) regime, with the seriousness that befits the last convulsion of a class desperately hanging on after its time had run out. Julien, in fact, is insidiously drawn into the enemy camp by the considerable largesse of a devoted master, who paves his way by degrees (the blue coat, the cross, the diplomatic mission) into a kind of equality at the top. The progress of romance will tumble the marquis from an equanimity which stops short at the fond wish for bestowing on his daughter the stool of a duchess. Although Julien will wring from him the red coat of a cavalry officer, the charm is broken and the end in sight. The letter from Mme de Rênal turns the one into an offending underling, the other into an irate master drenched in the bitter taste of his humiliation. Eighteenth-century insouciance must bow before the humorless turmoil of nineteenth-century existence.

François Leuwen is a man possessed of a number of idiosyncrasies which make him stand out even amid Stendhal's *happy few:* he is an ironist who loves his son and endeavors to trust him like a man; he is a banker who laughs at money and makes a stab at politics for the sheer entertainment of it; he is deeply in love with his own wife, and nothing else truly matters to him. Leuwen's love for his son is laced with wholesome chaffing in true eighteenth-century fashion. "A son is a creditor[9] given us by nature," he would declare as he paid Lucien's debts.

Sometimes he would tease this creditor. "Do you know," he said to Lucien one day, "what will be engraved on your marble tombstone at Père-Lachaise, if we should have the misfortune of losing you? 'Siste viator! Here lies Lucien Leuwen, republican, who for two years waged ruthless war on new boots and cigars.' " (5-6)

This love further takes the fairly unconventional path of demanding faithful attendance on Opera dancers, and even on a lady whose unassailable virtue is only undermined by that prankish father's intervention, armed with a cabinet post for her husband. The siege which the father himself lays to the heart of that cold beauty, pursued too moodily and with too little conviction by his son, almost breaks down his precarious composure:

At last, after several minutes of indirect propositions which kept Madame Grandet on tenterhooks, M. Leuwen pronounced the following words in a low and deeply emotional tone:

"Madame, I confess that I cannot bring myself to like you, for, because of you, my son will certainly die of consumption." And he thought with amusement: "My voice stood me in good stead, it has just the right note of pathos."

But, after all, M. Leuwen was not made to be a great diplomat, a Talleyrand, an ambassador to serious personages. Boredom made him ill-humored, and he was never sure that he would be able to resist the temptation of launching some amusing or insolent sally by way of diversion. After speaking his solemn line, he felt such an irresistible desire to laugh that he quickly fled. (*Telegraph,* 297-98)

There is an impish gleam in that father's eye that clearly designates him as far younger in spirit than the too often dejected young man over whom he watches with such original solicitude.

The truth is that the eighteenth century, glimpsed by young Beyle in the sprightly gait of Dr. Henri Gagnon and the sunny, all-conquering disposition of his carefree ladies' man son Romain, dispensed even in its decline an aura of playful victoriousness that made the age of Ossian, Manfred, and René appear by contrast like broken old age. Of the eighteenth century François Leuwen had the lucid irony and the cult of *volupté,* though it consisted of that rarefied kind that expresses itself by amusing conversation among choice friends over rare wines gracing an exquisitely appointed table. His love for Mme Leuwen itself partakes of the character of those famed eighteenth-century liaisons, more sacred by far than marriage, and which took on the appearance of a lifelong courtship the outcome of which could never be taken for granted. Mme Leuwen's love clearly goes to her son: her husband is kept youthful and sprightly by the need to watch over his fragile though successful rival, whose perverse radical inclinations endanger a life to which his own is thus indirectly tied. Lucien's death would kill his mother: such is the almost libertine reasoning that guarantees his father's lively interest in his welfare.

But if the banker Leuwen is a true scion of the *ancien régime,* unlike M. de La Mole he is descended not from its great court figures but from its financiers. The supreme miracle in Stendhal's sympathetic portrayal of Leuwen is that he salutes in him a man whose great power is tied up with the money he himself continued to make. Money, in Leuwen's case, acts as liberation from the shibboleths of title and decoration to which even a man of M. de La Mole's eminence and wit finds himself still enthralled. He is the only one of Stendhal's great men whose authority does not derive from membership in the landed military caste that had ruled Europe since the days of Charlemagne. As a great banker, privy to the sordid maneuvers of the government in power, Leuwen has both the wealth and the influence to thumb his nose at the Establishment with impunity, and his mordant wit, when he condescends to take part in the game of politics, poses a major threat to the survival of the cabinet. By concentrating in one man the gift of moneymaking and the ability to care for all the finer things to which moneymaking generally blinds a man, Stendhal created in Leuwen the true modern aristocrat, whose talents are characteristically unharnessed to larger ends. The *insouciance* that makes up the charm of the banker's character renders him unfit to undertake the boring task of reforming society. Having led him within sight of a cabinet post, Stendhal, with telling abruptness kills him off. It need come as no surprise that the affairs of this regal man are in a chaotic state: his debts very nearly balance his considerable assets—for what is money for, if not to be kept flowing?

Conte Mosca's title goes back beyond 1400. He fought in Spain under the French, and yet he ends up as the Conservative Prime Minister of Parma, with the reputation of a scourge of so-called Liberals (though this term, as we have seen, has a quite amazing range). The contradictions abound in that most complex of characters. His convictions are libertarian, yet he serves a despot faithfully and well. He is a military man, capable of stern action, yet he loathes the shedding of blood, and stakes his position on minimizing repression. He believes in *killing the devil before the devil kills you:* yet in a situation where corruption is the order of the day, he manages as Prime Minister to remain a poor and honest man. His title relates him to La Mole, his disinterestedness is an echo of Leuwen's own freedom from the thrall of power and pelf, but the unique conjunction of cynical toughmindedness and almost womanly delicacy contributes an Italian variation on the theme of political lucidity.

Physically

Mosca might have been forty or forty-five; he had strongly marked features, with no trace of self-importance, and a simple and light-hearted manner which was greatly in his favour; he would have looked very well indeed, if a whim on the part of his Prince had not obliged him to wear powder in his hair as a proof of his soundness in politics.   (Anchor, 101-2)

Such as he is he falls in love with Gina, the widow of a general who also served under Napoleon, and with whom he shares a love for the new freedom proclaimed across the Alps, the boldness to defy poverty that marks these scions of ancient families as authentically free spirits, and a playful disposition thanks to which power and favor fail to be converted into grimace and frown.

The partnership of Gina and Mosca is sealed, significantly, by the barefaced purchase of the title of Duchessa Sanseverina-Taxis, in exchange for the decent removal of the elderly ducal bridegroom on a long-coveted ambassadorship. To be in Parma Gina must be married and titled, and a power in her own right. The delicacy of a lover must not be confused with the cloudy scrupulosity of a Northern conscience!

Fabrizio's ecclesiastical honors are likewise the fruit of Conte Mosca's cool-headed realism, splendidly free of all Pecksniffian hypocrisy. The taint of revolutionary ardor and the capacity for action had to be expiated and forgotten if this young refugee from the Austrian police state was to survive and prosper in Parma: what better proof of a change of heart than the taking of holy orders? The rank of Archbishop, which was within the Conte's reach to bestow, was not unworthy of a scapegrace del Dongo, surely . . . . To bring up the sin of simony was of as little point, under the circumstances, as it was unlikely to cross the mind of either man, so honest and pure were their intentions essentially: i.e., to survive, with a minimum of vileness, amid the venomous spiders bred by absolute rule in a pocket-sized kingdom. Gina's unacknowledged passion for her nephew puts Mosca's tutelage of Fabrizio to a severe test, which only the younger man's own tactfulness, his pursuit of young actresses, and later his great love for Clelia manage to defuse. The poisoning of the ruling prince, undertaken unbeknownst to him as part of Gina's revenge, rouses Mosca to exhilarating exertions. Unwilling to let the widowed princess be endangered by the mob, he gallantly takes charge of the troops defending the palace, thwarting revolution from a curious sense of *noblesse oblige.* The role of savior of the dynasty is not one that can be sustained with much safety around a newly-enthroned prince who may have good reason to feel himself patronized. Conte Mosca soon leaves for exile in Naples, where he marries Gina to live in a modest retirement from which his irreplaceable talents cause him, in due course, to be recalled. He has been disabused by such buffetings, for the last line of the novel pronounces him immensely rich, while the prisons of Parma, under his wise management, are empty.

The figure of this benevolent potentate, too decent and too wise to take over the throne and play the part of an enlightened despot, probably sums up as well as any in his work Stendhal's ambivalent worship at the eighteenth-century altar: torn between the somber unreasonableness of political arrangements and the passionate unreasonableness symbolized by Gina (who returns his love but breathes only for Fabrizio), the noble, sensible, lucid Mosca steers his uneasy course, with a minimum of regrettable violence, with the maximum of felicity manageable under inclement skies.

CHAPTER 5

Brief Candle

Dominique's horror of the long inflated sentences fashionable in 1830 drove him into the jarring, the abrupt, the broken, the harsh.
—Note in Stendhal's hand in the margin of his copy of *Le Rouge et le Noir*.

FOLLOWING the death of Clelia Conti, Fabrizio's retirement to the Charterhouse of Parma and the subsequent fate of all the principals in this tangled tale take up no more than three paragraphs in half a page. Such a slapdash ending gave the author some qualms, and he laid the blame at the publisher's door, as his unwillingness to bring out the work in three volumes resulted in that excessive foreshortening. Though the case may be extreme it is by no means unrepresentative. Earlier critics caviled at the pistol shot with which Julien abruptly brings his career to an end, seeing in this unannounced decision a psychological inconsistency which some of them ascribe to the writer's need to adhere to the life of his model, the seminarian Berthet, an account of whose trial Stendhal must have read in *La Gazette des Tribunaux*.[1] *Lucien Leuwen*,[2] *Lamiel, Le Rose et le Vert* are unfinished; *Armance* concludes enigmatically with Octave's suicide at the height of what should have proven happiness, followed in the last sentence of the book by the information that his beloved mother and his bride Armance had taken the veil on the same day. But perhaps the three sentences with which Stendhal closes the tale of Mina de Vanghel, who shoots herself when Larçay stalks out of the house, define the spirit of the Stendhalian finale most tellingly: "Was her life a miscalculation? Her happiness had lasted eight months. She had too much mettle to put up with the reality of life."

The hero's life is expendable, the heroic life is not. That seems to be the meaning of the inevitable tragedy which swallows up the hero or the heroine at the end of the tale, and yet evokes no tears. We do not mourn the passing of Julien Sorel, whose head is lovingly interred by Mathilde in a ceremonial that makes of him a Renaissance nobleman, any more than we weep for Fabrizio del Dongo, immured in his cell after a short lifetime of the headiest adventures, spanning the days from the battle of Waterloo, backward in time to the escape of Alexander Farnese from the Castel Sant'Angelo. The hero's own body is an empty shell, regardless of his youth, once the cycle of his *gesta,* of his high deeds in the service of a noble destiny, crowned by love discovered, has run its meteoric course.

The question of *destiny,* precisely, is a vexing one for the young man born in the early days of the nineteenth century. Werther, Obermann, René propose a listless, defeated model. Napoleon's adventure streaked through his childhood horizon, fulfilling the hopes of the Revolution by exploding them, putting all things in question and leaving no usable answers. The Romantics found themselves grappling with the problem of a viable heroic stance in an age given over to the leveling realities of slow democratization, brought on by the combined impact of industrial revolution and middle-class rule. Balzac resorted to extra-rational powers, or to the secret society (the banding together of thirteen superior men, whose union put the world in their hands). Hugo rhapsodized over the underdog, dreaming of a hero risen from the dregs of society to redeem it through his love. Stendhal steers clear of the strong man mystique on the Right and of the laicized Man of Sorrows on the Left. The heroic life arises for him from a temperament impatient of lies; passionately devoted to that avoidance of every kind of meanness signified by the word *honor;* ignorant of the wiles by which smaller men secure a place in the sun; anxious in fact not to improve his lot at another's expense. His libertarian convictions spring from that quixotic fear; his innocence, like Parsifal's, wins him the Holy Grail of love; his fastidiousness marks him out for universal misunderstanding—no friend to the fickle mob, he is a fit companion only for the *happy few.* It cannot be claimed that this model offers a *solution* to the problem of the nineteenth-century hero—that contradiction in terms, a bourgeois hero! It has the eminent merit, however, of presenting the heroic life in its true *problematic* light. A final reconsideration of the three major stages in the Stendhalian canon of the heroic destiny may help us sort out some of the threads in that arresting tangle.

I *Julien at the Crossroads*

Ideology, that word grown thin and lackluster from overuse, is perhaps the most fitting term for what Julien Sorel understood by political commitment. Of the three great novels *The Red and the Black* is the one that most fully presses upon its hero the necessity of such a commitment—on the level of theory, i.e. as the ability to visualize his situation politically—on pains of literal obliteration. Not only to *become* but to *be* someone Julien Sorel must lift up his gaze from the crushing immediacies (his father's little gray eyes, his own inaptitude for heavy physical labor) to a kind of detached understanding of his situation in terms of a conflict of forces vastly beyond his puny self and all the redoubtable personages of his acquaintance. The surgeon-major's breathless tales fell not only upon the ears of a little boy drinking in the romance of the battlefield, but also on the ripe understanding of a child who could calculate the bearing of Napoleon's great deeds upon his own affairs. The victories that caused the thrones of Europe to totter on their absolutist foundations were the victories of a gifted commoner, leading the armies of a nation that had overthrown the old order, in which *birth* was all. Those victories rang the death-knell of hereditary greatness, while they ushered in the age of *personal* greatness: of talent, of energy, of will—the very marrow of his own being! The carpenter's son had a personal stake in the French Revolution: it handed over to the likes of himself the key to epic achievement. He owed Napoleon Bonaparte the further debt of a supremely realized exemplar of what the Revolution was about, and of the warlike stance that alone could pluck its fruits. Every common soldier, in the great man's words, held in his knapsack a marshal's baton. The Revolution had spawned a million foes: the old order would not go down in a single battle. But it had marked unmistakably one's friends and one's enemies (the corridors of History are full of echoes!): the battle lines were drawn up by the ideological fields of force, separating into two hermetically sealed camps the men ranged under the banner of achieve-ment and those grimly hanging on to superior might and existing arrangements, the forces of the Future and the forces of the Past.

Julien's commitment must be called ideological, in part because it rests on a grasp of the larger issues raised by his Napoleonic hero worship, in part because, as we have seen, it is entirely divorced from all political machinery, and hence cannot lead to political action. The acuteness of his estimate of the underlying ideological factors stands revealed in his recognition of the central role of the Church, acting as the intellectual powerhouse of the regime since the Restoration of the Bourbons. The vision of the bishop of Agde, no older than himself, frowning into the mirror as he rehearses the sign of the cross, confirms Julien in his choice of the cassock as the wings upon which talent must rise in an age of hypocrisy, without detracting from the heroic abnegation of such a choice. Camouflage too is called for in war. But the hero's resolve, even guided by the eagle perspicacity of superior intelligence, is no match for a millennial institution garnering the sharpest minds and the keenest wills in Europe in the service of a sanctified ideology, cheerfully waved aloft by those whose consciences are most unburdened by its commands. Julien's faltering success at the Besançon seminary gives proof that the essential solitude of the heroic life condemns the man who would do the work of History to dismount and struggle in the mass like a common soldier, or face ignominious annihilation.

As Don Quixote had shown plainly in the loss of his grinders and the battering of his barber's basin helmet long before Julien had ever been heard of, the heroic life in an age of iron is mostly a source of humiliation and grief. The most strenuous exertions, the loftiest hopes, the boldest calculations may pave the road to the executioner's blade for a man reviled, moreover, as a faithless priest, a small-time seducer, a traitor to his benefactors. Nothing more is required than a single slip on the arduous path, but success is more perilous by far! Lieutenant Julien Sorel de la Vernaye earned his spurs but lost even the memory of his mission. To triumph alone, as the hero must, he must either raise his visor and court instant annihilation, as the lone subversive who dreams of lifting the heedless masses into their inheritance; or, as Julien discovered too late, he finds himself hugged so close by those he must challenge that his successful camouflage now adheres to his skin; for to deal with the mighty of the earth a man must be as one of them. Hence Julien's ideological quest for greatness leads him into the impasse out of which his second, his romantic self must now extricate him.

The romantic destiny of the carpenter's son Julien Sorel reflects a double truth in matters of the heart: the crown goes to the man who does not truly seek it; and the dream world into which love's elect must needs step may very well be the dream of another. The "conquest" of Mme de Rênal illustrates the first proposition, marriage with Mathilde is the unlooked-for consequence of the second.

The heroic life is a life of the will. Romantic entanglement is notoriously a matter of unpremeditated election, hence the not altogether fortuitous semantic confusion that links Romanticism—as a historically determined modality of thought and feeling—with the affairs of the heart. Romanticism is among other things an acknowledgment that the will must bow to the fatum of strong feelings, that the heart vouchsafes more than Pascal's *raisons que la raison ne connaît pas:* a direct intuition of a higher truth, implanted there by the Creator. The originality of Stendhal's adherence to this Revelation is found in the indissoluble connection he established between the presence *of the strongest will* and its ultimate transcendence. Unlike René, Adolphe, Olympio, or even Corinne, his heroes are not seized upon by a passion against which nothing in their lives stood out to defend them—more or less willing victims of a fate that dragged them down to their death or to desolation. Julien, Lucien, Fabrizio have this in common that all have some good reason to resist love, and that out of this tension of the will true love arises and lifts them into that easeful death only dreamt of by the poet.

Julien's case in that respect marks off the extreme. His ignorance is bottomless, his daring infinite—but in a cause that is utterly foreign to the matter in hand. He undertakes the conquest of Mme de Rênal with a literal-mindedness worthy of that paragon of bookish knights, Don Quixote, because it was his duty as a soldier in the invisible army of the Revolution to do so. The call to arms of a will that imbues his frail person with grandeur finds an echo in the breast of a woman as capable of savoring greatness as she is unused to finding it in her own surroundings. The valor of a man in the frame of a child operates the miracle of strength-in-weakness whereby a woman's heart surrenders. Julien lands in full battle gear in the soft bed where love takes his ease, but unlike Paris similarly wafted into Helen's chamber from the battlefield of Ilion, his reception is a gentle one and his transfiguration fully earned. None but the brave deserve the fair: the lion-hearted boy who knows of love but what he read about it in Rousseau's *Confessions*—that grand master of virile ineptitude—comes into his lover's reward largely because he knew not to what place he stumbled. Invincible ignorance shields him against temptation: not having sought a prize, but merely having reached for a weapon in the war he knows himself to be engaged in, he vaults himself at one leap into the bliss lovingly prepared for him by his creator. Reciprocated love, that elusive object of the Romantic pilgrimage, comes to him almost at once, unbidden, stamping his existence with the seal of a higher purpose.

The conquest of Mathilde, on the other hand, exhibits his romantic destiny in another light altogether. Mathilde, like her predecessor, is attracted to Julien by the somber hue of resolution that plays over the pale and silent young provincial in her father's employ. The suspected depths she divines under his haughty demeanor take on in her mind a "romantic" coloration, in the literary sense of that word this time. Mme de Rênal was genuine and unread: her reaction to Julien's heroic stature was intuitive and unmediated by fiction or cliché. Mathilde is incurably bookish, though she is no Emma Bovary (she has no need to expiate an obscure fate vicariously!). Her *Mémorial* is the account of the exploits of the great men of her own lineage,[3] and she renders a cult to that Boniface de La Mole beheaded under Charles IX for his part in a rebellious skirmish, whose remarkably beautiful head had been buried in secret by the lady he loved, *la reine* Marguerite (Margaret of Valois). Julien Sorel gains his ascendancy over her by a play of her own imagination, sparked by his conversation with the picturesque outlaw Count Altamira. She is caught between the excitement of seeing in him a foe worthy of herself, "a modern Danton," and the realization that the energy of a Boniface de La Mole is now to be sought in vain amid the exquisite gentlemen of her own class, appalled at any gesture or thought not thoroughly rehearsed beforehand; that it could only lodge in the heart of a future tribune of the people, a Julien Sorel. The dreamer Sorel thus finds himself imprisoned in the dream of another: Mathilde loves in him the perfect knight of her own imagination, part Danton, part Boniface de La Mole. His secret mission, deflated by her enthusiastic endorsement, runs aground altogether in consequence of his "naturalization" into the class where her great name cannot help but take him, willing or not. It is high time that Mme de Rênal return him to himself by her cruel intervention: only the surgeon's knife could have severed Lieutenant de la Vernaye from the alien and erratic dream that threatened to swallow him whole.

The hero's salvation brings to an improbable close his unique life experience, answering the call of his destiny with the most impressive leap of all. Ideologically Julien's life is a cruel impasse; romantically, it ends up in that least enviable of all dilemmas: caught between two women whose claims on him are equally strong. The double constriction is broken by the method perfected of yore by Alexander the Great: the swish of a blade (set in motion by the shooting of a pistol) cuts through the Gordian knot by lifting the hero's career to a third, a metaphysical level, where life's contradictions are resolved in the acceptance of death.

The death of Mme de Rênal from the shot fired at her by Julien as she knelt in the church of Verrières might have solved the hero's dilemma in the reckless manner of a Romantic epilogue: recognizing that the only woman he truly loved could never be his any more the hero slays her, to expire on her corpse, reunited in death at last, though torn asunder in life. The falseness of this pose is spared Julien by the sincerity of his own body: he loves Mme de Rênal too much not to shake as he fires, he misses, and the second bullet merely wounds her. Life's untidiness comes to the rescue of the hero. Having failed to take the life of the beloved, Julien is faced, furthermore, with the determined conspiracy mounted by Mathilde, enlisting the aid of friend and foe, of the good Fouqué and of the sinister Frilair (reached by the long arm of Mme de Fervaques), to win his acquittal. To earn his release from a life tainted by failure, a life that has not measured up to the soldierly standards held up to him by the ghost of Napoleon, Julien Sorel must practically wrest the death sentence from a jury half-intimidated, half-suborned, by the splendidly irrelevant address in which he taunts them for their persecution of the likes of himself—those sons of the people whose only crime is to aspire above their station. His foiled *crime passionnel* is thus lifted to the level on which, obscurely, it had been intended: respecting the life of Mme de Rênal, which he cherished more than his own, the shot was aimed at the heart of that Establishment on which the humble carpenter's son had long ago declared total war.

Prison is a privileged setting for the Stendhalian hero. It provides Julien (as it will Fabrizio unreservedly) with that elevated solitude—his cell is at the top of a keep—which Proust was to describe as one of the requirements of his sensibility.[4] But the quite literal uplift he receives (alongside some inevitably uneasy moments) from his isolation *au-dessus de la mêlée,* his forcible disentanglement from the increasingly confused role he had been called upon to play as La Mole's emissary and son-in-law-to-be, give but a feeble foretaste of the bliss he is to know once his life has been contemptuously flung in the balance, and lost as it were with joyful defiance. The gospel saying which Gide too one day will make his own, *"Qui veut sauver sa vie la perdra"* here takes on a singularly laicized meaning, but it spiritualizes nonetheless the Romantic absolutization of love. Freed by his example of all the scruples that belong to the worldly side of existence, Mme de Rênal joins her would-be assassin in his cell, blissfully oblivious of position, reputation, and even elementary decency. Her children are forgotten, Mathilde brushed aside: the two lovers commune in an embrace earned by total renunciation. The meaning of life, if that isn't too pompous a phrase, stands revealed before Julien once he has divested himself of all worldly preoccupation, stepping, like a monk, into a cell where the sole presence that ever wholly took him out of himself extends her ephemeral-eternal embrace.

It is noteworthy that Julien gives belief in God serious consideration on only two occasions, the second of which comes at this point. His first doubt comes when he is faced with Mme de Rênal's despair at the illness of her son, which she imputes to her own sinfulness: "So that's what adultery means! he said to himself. . . . Could it be possible that these deceitful priests are right? That they who commit so many sins themselves are privileged to know the true theory of sin? What a grotesque idea! . . . *(Quelle bizarrerie!)"* (130) *There are more things in heaven and earth, Horatio. . . .* Julien does not linger over the thought, but that he should entertain it at all reveals a chink in his positivistic armor, deepened further upon the present occasion. Reflecting on man's notorious untrustworthiness after his father's visit to the death cell, Julien dares even to shake his idol, Napoleon, guilty himself of "charlatanism"!

Where lies Truth? . . . In religion? . . . Yes, he added, with the bitter smile of supreme contempt, in the mouths of the Maslons, the Frilairs, the Castanèdes. . . . Perhaps in true Christianity, whose priests are possibly paid no more than were the apostles! . . .

Ah! if there were a true religion. . . . Fool that I am! I see a Gothic cathedral, stained glass windows centuries old. My fainting heart dreams of the priest who is pictured in those windows. . . . My soul would understand him, my soul has need of him. . . . I find only a conceited fool with greasy hair, a Chevalier de Beauvoisis, in fact, without his charm. . . . But a true priest, after all. . . . Then loving hearts would have some common meeting-place on earth. . . . We should not be isolated. This good priest would speak to us of God. But what God? Not the God of the Bible, a petty despot, cruel, and athirst for vengeance . . . but Voltaire's God, just, kind, and infinite. . . .

He was troubled by all his memories of that Bible which he knew by heart. . . . But how, he thought, as soon as *two or three are gathered together* can one believe in this great name of GOD, after the frightful abuse that our priests make of it? (501-2)

Enlightenment skepticism wins out in the end and Julien shakes himself out of this "unwholesome" reverie by an appeal to the life of *duty* (italicized by Stendhal) which in his own case testifies to a transcendent principle untouched by priestly malice. But the yearning for a Truth beyond human machinations, and the sober acknowledgment that sin is a reality to be reckoned with in human existence give proof of a sensibility attuned to mysteries repudiated by the age of Voltaire. The faith of Julien Sorel is not to be sought in his utterances: he is too tender of God's own honor to join those who bend His Name to their will. A knight, in the last analysis, is to be known by his deeds. Heroism supposes a heavenly dimension of which the heart of Mme de Rênal is all the proof a man could need.

II *The Stalemate*

Julien Sorel's career rounds the tale of a heroic quest successful beyond all expectation. The unfinished state of the novel *Lucien Leuwen* testifies to an even more arduous imaginative undertaking: the depiction of a quest doomed to relative failure. The setting, the nature of the obstacles, the character of the foes Lucien is called upon to measure himself against, all play their part in defining heroic failure. Reared to wealth and ease, spurred on by his predicament to *serve* rather than *fight* the existing order, unable to emulate, despise, or overcome an all-powerful benevolent father, the hero needs the bracing gifts of financial ruin and exile for the chance to break free of a fate that cloys him with unlooked-for kindness. To be unhorsed in the sight of the beloved is the allegory of his particular way. Like all Stendhalian heroes he must lose his life in order to save it, but the loss, in his case, is that of wealth and dignity, since unkind fate saddled him from the cradle with an excess of both.

Nancy, Paris, Italy are the three stages of his quest. The last remains shrouded in the mystery of things uncreated, but we may read in the book of Beyle's own life that a modest diplomatic post in Italy is the key to the freedom of a man who has learned to be content with the fulfillment of half his wishes; who reserves the right to live and dream with some abandon, while sacrificing the hope of seeing his countrymen rise up for their own right to liberty and happiness. In a world of fools, knaves, and scoundrels some respite is to be gained by putting a distance between oneself and those scoundrels closest to one, and therefore most objectionable—rejoicing in the amused contemplation of the knaves of another land, whose antics are softened by sunshine and music. Mme de Chasteller undoubtedly will make her way to that land of diminished scruples and lowered inhibitions, and her greatly overestimated defenses will crumple before Lucien's much weathered inexperience. And the end will come, no doubt, with its customary abruptness.

But in Nancy the end is nowhere in sight, it is just the highly unpromising beginning. Gloom, tortuousness, the threat of slights and even dishonor hover over the most desolate landscape in France: the interminable Eastern plain. The army no longer answers to the dream of heroic endeavor in a setting of virile amity, such as Napoleon's stirring adventure might have suggested to a youth barely twenty in the early 1830s. To be sure Lucien entered the service somewhat wryly,[5] and that in itself was a strange thing to do for a boy expelled from Polytechnique for his republican convictions. But the Republic is a virtuous bore. Lucien's heart is young, and magenta pipings are hard to quarrel with: if no spurs are to be earned in the Lancers these days, one may rightly despair of attaining manhood at all. Quite aside from the snubs, the general sordidness, the highly unheroic billiard-playing character of garrison existence, Lucien discovers the most bitter contradiction between his youthful aspirations and the true nature of a peacetime army under an unpopular bourgeois regime: the army's proper function is that of an auxiliary state police, geared to the repression of the working class, strictly enjoined at the time from the formation of any labor unions.[6] While he is spared the full execution of a duty impossible to reconcile with his political convictions or even with simple humanity, Lucien does not escape the irony of a commitment to greatness which exposes him to thinly disguised criminality.

Nancy further confronts him with the grotesque reversals to which the accidents of history so cheerfully expose all political principles. The army, in Nancy, is caught in the crossfire of the jeers of the young (who worship the Republic) and the snubs of the leading citizens (fiercely devoted to the fortunes of the exiled Charles X). The old nobility unanimously bar their doors to the uniformed servants of the lesser Orléans branch of the Capetian family. In consequence, those whose very existence is bound up with power and the military find themselves voluntarily excluded from either, out of loyalty to a dream of reinstated absolute sway utterly denied them by the march of history. And it is in this almost insanely shut-off and backward-looking milieu, amid what he himself sneeringly terms "those country comedians," that Lucien (as will one day Henry James's Newman in *The American)* finds the rose grown on that dung heap, the ineffable Mme de Chasteller, whose Divine Right outlook is as unclouded by self-serving practicalities as are his own republican convictions. Lucien falls in love, as do all Stendhalian heroes, across the chasm of party. Though his love is returned, the iron law of his fate, reflecting the inner truth of an age of impotence (Louis-Philippe, the nobles, the workers, Lucien share in it alike) ordains his defeat and deception at the hands of the evil dwarf Du Poirier, whose wiles more than overmatch Lucien's youthful inexperience.

The July monarchy is the image of a world set topsy-turvy. The king's scepter is a furled umbrella, the overthrow of feudal reaction signals an era of "progress" characterized by immobilism, the service of the State is the swiftest way to gain the contempt of the people. Mme de Chasteller is as chaste as her name implies, yet Lucien first hears of her as the mistress of a departed lieutenant colonel, ascribing her reserve with him solely to the absence of the proper epaulettes; and he lets himself be driven from her side in despair by an elaborately staged confinement, mounted for his benefit by the resourceful Du Poirier. Misunderstanding reigns supreme, giving the old and wicked the power to hoodwink and disarm the trusting and the youthful.

The Parisian stage of Lucien's probation conforms to an equally deceptive pattern. Although he now lives in Paris, the main theater of his exploits lies in the provinces, where as the Minister's troubleshooter Lucien must beard the all-powerful prefects in their dens. His duties in the capital are largely confined to an ornamental pose as the confirmed unhappy lover of Mme Grandet, while he also cultivates an Opera dancer on the side. Father's orders. One might as easily say: doctor's orders, since the erotic is here conceived of as a sub-branch of therapeutic science. Falseness on all sides (except for the dancer: *le naturel se réfugie chez les danseuses,* thinks Lucien): Lucien is not in love with Mme Grandet, in fact he detests her emphatically (the cure belongs to the family of bitter pills). Mme de Chasteller is his only love, and by her side Mme Grandet, with her airs, her loveless self-regard, in spite of her great beauty is no more than a gaily painted toad. Lucien pays her court *to conceal* his undying true passion, much as Henri Beyle had posed, on his return to Paris dismissed from Métilde's side, as a man too hardboiled ever to have drawn a lover's sigh. The universal deception is compounded once more, however, as the terrible Leuwen *père* engineers Mme Grandet's surrender (a bit of staging as skillfully and stealthily done as Du Poirier's, and quite as devastating in its own turnabout way). Lucien's "victory" turns into his humiliation, the cold-hearted beauty then melts in her turn—foisting upon her victor the distasteful role of a cad.

The sentimental confusion on the Paris scene matches the labyrinthine tortuousness of Lucien's daytime endeavors. Having failed as a soldier he tries his hand as a highly-placed and solidly-backed civil servant, bent on the truly Herculean endeavor of serving in the Augean stables while keeping his honor intact. His career is a string of victories, each one of which would sink a less formidably connected man out of sight. He purchases the silence of the agent Kortis, done to death in a bit of governmental secret dirty work, by a pension paid out to the widow; but he tells the War Minister exactly what he thinks of him, offering to trade bullets into the bargain. He stakes both his credit and a large sum of the government's money on buying off the pro-Bourbon opposition in a local election, to form a coalition that would deny a prominent Liberal a sure-fire victory. The ire of a too-openly flouted prefect defeats his scheme by an unforeseeable Kamikaze charge (by denying him his victory the prefect seals his own fate). But the Stendhalian Providence that watches over the endearingly inept (or if you will, those who are too noble to succeed) is hard at work in this novel. In fact, the banker François Leuwen, that benevolent omnipotent father, more than makes up with his gold and his lethal wit for all his son's haughty blunders. In a reversal that threatens to upset the expected course of the novel, this overly ebullient personage steps into what by rights should be the place of his son. Elected deputy (having entered the race for a lark), he fashions a political bloc, rocks the Cabinet by his telling jibes, is called in to the Château so the King himself may take his measure. The last straw in Lucien's difficult struggle to fight free of the treacle sea of his overwhelming good fortune is to have his father run away with the novel whose hero he himself is supposed to be! Hence the perhaps not altogether surprising news, before the sudden death of that overwhelming figure, that Lucien suffered from an inability to feel much liking for him!

François Leuwen is cut down just as his second youth threatened to pose an insuperable obstacle to his son's emancipation. The abruptness of his end, in fact, marks how close he came to usurping the hero's fate altogether. Therein precisely lies the originality of this unfinished novel, and the rather modern character of the hero's predicament. Unlike Julien and Fabrizio, Lucien is given no foes to threaten his life and his liberty: his danger comes almost solely from his friends. The bourgeois hero must conquer in a world made soft and resistless by opulence and complicity. He must largely invent his challenges and create his hardships. Lucien's first steps into the arena of his freedom are taken when he turns down the chance to save half his fortune by declaring a blandly matter-of-course bankruptcy (urged upon him by the gray-haired chief accountant in his father's firm). He leaves himself almost penniless to repay the creditors in full, thus bending his fate to the heroic nakedness overkind Fortune steadfastly denied.

III *Volunteer to Archbishop*

Fabrizio is in a sense the most mysterious of Stendhal's heroes. Julien is opaque to the Rênals and the La Moles who have no way of divining his obscure self-invented mission. Lucien, by and large, is transparent to himself and to others, caught in contradictions that are not of his own making and which he strives vainly to reconcile. Fabrizio, on the other hand, exhibits a most un-French confusion of backward ignorance and refinement of taste, utter frivolity and highest seriousness, unashamed feudal arrogance and a most unthinking dedication to the "wave of the future" that would wash his kind away. In creating an *Italian* character Stendhal was careful to remove from it that *self*-consciousness which to him was a hateful feature of French existence, thus depriving Fabrizio of that capacity for a review of his inner resources whereby Julien especially, and to some extent Lucien, maintain at all times a kind of military preparedness in their martial souls. Fabrizio's one great meditation on his own nature, while confined in the *campanile* for a whole day on his secret visit to Priore Blanès, runs the following haphazard course:

Happiness carried him to an exaltation of mind quite foreign to his nature; he considered the incidents of life, he, still so young, as if already he had arrived at its farthest goal. "I must admit that, since I came to Parma," he said to himself at length after several hours of delicious musings, "I have known no tranquil and perfect joy such as I used to find at Naples in galloping over the roads of Vomero or pacing the shores of Miseno. All the complicated interests of that nasty little court have made me nasty also. . . . I even believe that it would be a sorry happiness for me to humiliate my enemies if I had any; but I have no enemy. . . . Stop a moment!" he suddenly interjected, "I have got an enemy, Giletti. . . . And here is a curious thing," he said to himself, "the pleasure that I should feel in seeing such an ugly fellow go to all the devils in hell has survived the very slight fancy that I had for little Marietta. . . ."

... "I should perhaps have done well to adopt the *caffè* life, as the Duchessa said; she seemed to incline in that direction, and she has far more intelligence than I. Thanks to her generosity ... I should always have a horse and a few scudi to spend on digging and collecting a cabinet. Since it appears that I am not to know the taste of love, there will always be those other interests to be my great sources of happiness; I should like, before I die, to go back to visit the battlefield of Waterloo and try to identify the meadow where I was so neatly lifted from my horse and left sitting on the ground. That pilgrimage accomplished, I should return constantly to this sublime lake; nothing else as beautiful is to be seen in the world, for my heart at least. Why go so far afield in search of happiness? It is here, beneath my eyes!" (Anchor, 171-72)

Such the meandering course of the hero's self-knowledge—made up mostly of ingenuous awe at the depth of his self-ignorance.

A broken course is indeed to be the hallmark of Fabrizio's heroic endeavor. His dash to Waterloo as a sixteen-year-old volunteer on the side of the French, with whom General Pietranera, the husband of his beloved Aunt Gina, had himself served, breaks with all the realities amid which he is fated to lead his short life: Austrian rule, feudal privilege, medieval political backwardness. Plunged as a raw youth in one of the telling historical moments on the stage of world affairs, he is characteristically unable to make out with certainty that he has been on a battlefield at all. Yet the event marks him nonetheless decisively, condemning him to betrayal by his own father (backing Ascanio's gesture) and lifelong exile from the beloved shores of Lake Como. Exile from Milan, followed by exile from Parma, forces upon him the listless existence of a refugee, who must pay court to a Neapolitan Duchessa ("Good God, how bored I have been during the long assignations that fair Duchessa used to accord me!") or elope with an actress or a singer, to signify to the watchful authorities the proper measure of harmless frivolity. The most spectacular break of all lies of course in the trammeling up of this dashing cavalier in the robes of ecclesiastical high office, perhaps a leap that is even greater than Julien's sacrificial choice of the black cassock over the scarlet tunic. An archbishop who fought with the French at Waterloo, a future archbishop whose sermons famed far and wide are lures to secure a tryst with an elusive beloved indeed stretches all belief in the mutability of experience. There could be no more telling allegorization of the hazardous course of heroism in what Flaubert one day was to call *ce maudit dix-neuvième siècle!*

The contradictions Fabrizio is unable to ride out in any kind of smoothly coherent course (like Julien's, for instance, until the break at the end) are rooted deeper than even the disastrous Italian political scene would suggest: they arise from his very being. As a great nobleman with generous aspirations, Fabrizio is caught in one of history's least acceptable ironies: everything that goes to make of him a man impatient of oppression and injustice binds him inextricably to an order founded on oppression and injustice. As the bearer of a great name, Fabrizio learns the meaning of greatness in the storied deeds of his putative ancestors. The noble carelessness with which he sets out for Waterloo at the sign of an eagle's flight was learned from the example of dashing forebears. But valor in the service of freedom does not erase the consciousness of privilege. The right of an unsaintly youth to the mantle of a prince of the Church is assumed by him unquestioningly: the one time (on the shores of Lake Como) the realization of his position is allowed to appear before his mind in its ugly contradictoriness, it merely leaves in his mouth the ashen taste of things that cannot be swallowed nor spewed out. Yet to that, as it were, *objective* level of contradiction must be added, in Fabrizio's case, an even less manageable *subjective* level. This young refugee from Napoleon's army and from the vengefulness of his male kin soaked in pernicious absolutist doctrine, this innocent bystander who will soon fall victim to the machinations of courtiers anxious to placate the pride of a pigmy ruler, is himself convinced from the heart of the rightness of all such Divine Right twaddle imparted to him at the Naples seminary—so much so that the Prince of Parma takes an instant dislike to such a blatant comedian. But the fact of the matter is that Fabrizio adheres unthinkingly to the code of his own circle, with the same ingenuous faith as was displayed by that intransigent Carlist Mme de Chasteller: neither is moved by self-interest or calculated arrogance, both reflect in all simplicity—with no thought of privilege or oppression—the *felt* truth of their noble birth.

One can scarcely speak of an impasse in the face of a political situation so thoroughly removed from the mainstream of libertarian action, of an ideological orientation so thoroughly confused. Fabrizio's removal to the Farnese tower lifts him away from a morass by the side of which Julien's predicament appears practically Cartesian. Unlike his French counterpart, Fabrizio does not learn in prison to forego a course of political action rendered impracticable by a combination of character and circumstance. In his case political action *never was,* his life having been no more than a series of dashes for survival (after an initial *beau geste).* No, for Fabrizio immurement at the top of the tower, with only the sky, the clouds, Clelia and her aviary for companions, taught him the true nature of his destiny in this world: a life of contemplation. Rejoining the Petrarchan mode native to the skies under which he was born, Fabrizio discovers love in the swooning awareness of the presence of the beloved, sufficient unto itself—and thereby comes at last into his knightly inheritance. Life for him from that moment on revolves around a single object: to secure the presence of Clelia. All thoughts of fame or even survival fall from him like outworn garments: to be under the same roof as the beloved jailer's daughter he gladly rushes off to reoccupy his cell—after the meaningless interlude of an unprecedented escape.

The improbable closing phase of his worldly existence, by a complicated double irony, cloaks his true spiritual being in vestments that are only superficially usurped. Fabrizio weeps in his robes as the orchestra intones an aria of Cimarosa at a reception where the Marchesa Crescenzi is present:

"These violent headaches, when I do anything to thwart them, as I am doing this evening," he said to the General of the Minorites, "end in floods of tears which provide food for scandal in a man of my calling; and so I request Your Illustrious Reverence to allow me to look at him while I cry, and not to pay any attention."

"Our Father Provincial at Catanzaro suffers from the same disability," said the General of the Minorites. And he began in an undertone a long narrative. (474)

Subterfuge and incongruity melt into a kind of surrealistic rightness: this man who weeps for the loss of a woman he worships, when music translates him into a higher sphere of purified passion and remembered felicity, does less dishonor to his habit than half the schemers and inquisitors who in the eyes of the world have better title to wearing it. The eloquence of his sermons springs from the genuineness of his grief just as the austerity of his existence testifies to the cleansing presence of true love.

Clelia's vow puts the finishing touch to Fabrizio's destiny. Having sworn to the Madonna, in expiation of her complicity in the escape that brought her father dishonor, never to look again upon the face of her lover, when at last she yields to the preacher's fame and falls under the spell of his ardent declaration, she preserves her vow unbroken by trysting with Fabrizio in the dark only. By a kind of reversal of the myth of Psyche, Clelia both asserts and rebukes the proverbial frailty of woman, but in so doing she succeeds in immaterializing the love of Fabrizio decisively, returning even the act of physical fulfillment to its spiritual sense. Hence the poignancy of the lover's rebellion, who by taking physical possession of his own child, seeks to transform a purely spiritual union into a marriage, thereby shattering three lives which had their true being away from this world.

The hero's destination is the heaven, not of Calvin's elect, whose faithful labors on this earth are a mark of their election, but of *the happy few* who know that to be is better than to have, and learn that to love is more than to rule. The world in which they are fated to make their way is one that rewards their indifference to its values with persecution and infamy. It is the very love that Stendhal bears the radiant sons and daughters of his imagination that carries them so swiftly through the dark places where a dungeon spells freedom, to that bright flame in which the indifferent body is allowed to perish, releasing a soul rendered worthy of eternity by the service of love.

EPILOGUE

Fortune's Wheel

"I shall be understood around 1880." Calling the exact turn of the wheel of fortune is an apt exercise for the kind of wry equanimity that allows an author to toss off his masterpieces like so many tickets in the lottery of fame. Stendhal the ex-cavalry officer no doubt smiles in the heaven reserved for God's loving servants, the intractable atheists,[1] at the enviable accuracy with which he called his shot. Hippolyte Taine's enthusiastic essay dates back to 1864, but it is only a forerunner of an uninterrupted vogue quite decisively and perceptively epitomized by Paul Bourget's portrait in the *Essais de Psychologie contemporaine* in 1883. Bourget referred to him as a contemporary: he has retained that privileged standing for the better part of a century by now. In a day and age when relevance is all, the achievement is worth a second look.

There is much to be said for finding oneself hopelessly at odds with one's own time, when the age is given over to bombast and prudery. *Le naturel,* that touchstone of all classicism, is hard to come by when Frenchmen mistake themselves for old Romans, when over a span of four decades at least seven political regimes, ranging from absolute monarchy to radical republic, demand the loyalties, in quick succession, of all men prepared to prosper or even merely to survive, when MacPherson and the Gothic novel set the literary climate. A passion for veracity and simplicity—the worship of the cold muse Urania—is a dissonance to be valued in a concert of strained notes and artful dodges. The less he pleased Sainte-Beuve and Jules Janin, the better pleased we shall be with him ourselves.

Even so, the misunderstanding need not be exaggerated. Sainte-Beuve, the old fox, smelled out the instinctive reserve which led Stendhal to conceal a tender heart behind the cavalryman's rude sallies.[2] His quarrel with the writer was indeed quite fundamental: the cant, the false idealization, the prudent genuflexions in the direction of altar and throne were far too glaringly dispensed with for the taste of that official of

French letters. Stendhal need grieve at no failure on his part to "get through" to the keenest ear in the kingdom: his posthumous reburial by Sainte-Beuve amid the oddities of the age (an honor shared by Baudelaire—so much for critical prescience!) is the acknowledgment of what indeed he stands for—not so much the scourge (a grim and almost official-sounding function) as the freebooter of contemporary thought and letters.

Balzac, be it said to his eternal credit, saluted in the relatively obscure Stendhal the brother genius who authored *The Charterhouse of Parma*. His unreserved admiration, though couched in the ominous prose of a man for whom all is tortuous and abyssal in God's monstrous creation, was lavished on Stendhal not long before he departed these shores,[3] sweetening his exile from fame most opportunely. It is hard not to feel that the deity that presides over literary fortune is imbued with something of Stendhal's own smiling insouciant spirit when we consider the ironies concealed in the meeting of those two giants. Balzac's stature was assured then, as it is now, resting on the unexampled achievement of a vast and coherent creation. mirroring mankind as it worked and fought, while it built under his own gaze the intricate maze of a new industrial society. Armed with a mystique of power and achievement Balzac created a world infused with chaotic energies that fitted it to dispute the sway of the registry of deaths and births, *rivaliser avec l'état civil.* Regard and admiration for an achievement which has laid the groundwork for the growth of the modern novel, even taken together with the enduring fascination of a world in which, like Proust's M. de Guermantes, it is still possible to lose oneself with pleasure, have not preserved all parts of it against the ravages of time. To be a Balzacian today requires that one overlook the intolerable pretentiousness of the style, the plebeian vulgarity that throbs in the presence of power, the maudlin susurrations at the altar of Woman alternating with the crudest pseudo-physiological thinking (Mme de Mortsauf, heaven help us! dying of something dangerously akin to orgasmic deprivation), the deep ruminations that lead to a profession of faith in the political platform of Law and Order. Stendhal's rather casual bid for posthumous fame, resting on a string of unfinished and miscellaneous writings upon the sea of which sail a handful of inimitably graceful men-o'-war, has certainly overtaken and perhaps even put in the shadow the mountainous output of his formidable contemporary. Lightness of touch, swiftness of pace, acuteness of perception are qualities that have very much come into their own since the days when the pace of existence suited more ponderous expression. Proust's many-volumed monument to the combined Balzacian and Stendhalian modes gives proof, to be sure, that sheer mass is not altogether disavowed—but no rule can be drawn from a work in every particular exceptional.

At all events the revival of Stendhal's fame circa 1880 offers food for further meditation on the capriciousness of Fortune. Taine and Bourget drew a quite faithful likeness of the genius of a man both quick and reflective, tender and hardboiled. The trait that was singled out for their admiration by the analytic positivist spirit of their own day, however, was Stendhal's own analytic positivist side—his dryly cursive presentation of the small telling detail, his incisive grasp of psychological realities. Stendhal was reborn a forerunner of the schools of Realism and Naturalism headed by Zola and the Goncourts. The man who wryly set down all praise from literary men as so many certificates of resemblance was to owe to the fortuitous conjunction of a side of his own genius with the far narrower preoccupations of the writers of another day the measure of veneration which no doubt he was quite fortunate not to have had to put up with in his own time. All admiration skews, but manysidedness soon rights itself again, from the mere force of the currents of interests and taste which seize upon one after another of the multiple facets it offers.

Hence Nietzsche, though not much later in time than Taine, yet eons apart in the scope of his prophecy, heralds for the age of Gide and Malraux a Stendhal more attuned to a time "in love with profundity": the maker of masks, the master of the elusive self, the philosopher of the future. Lafcadio or Bernard breathe the same amused defiance as Lamiel, obey the same imperious code as the inflexible Julien. The doomed men of the Chinese and Spanish civil wars trudge on the side that to them spells freedom and dignity with the same unwavering loyalty that binds Stendhal's more devious heroes, caught in a less virulent predicament.

The universality of his appeal lies in part in the very primacy of the self, which to Stendhal was the object of a lifelong and ever-baffled fascination, and which through Barrès to Gide's heedless and Proust's tormented virtuosity came to dominate the whole landscape of modern preoccupation. The elusive, the protean, the autonomous self holds a very special fascination for an age so constituted technologically and demographically as to be faced with the nightmare of the extinction of the self, a nightmare righteously pursued as the highest goal of the social endeavor by a vast conglomerate of the world's population. The Enlightenment's faith in human reason was a faith in personal achievement (the man of good will, the *philosophe*). It shines through the resolve that arms the Stendhalian hero against both sloth and malice. Let a much later time stigmatize such a faith as both bourgeois and ineffectual: where men breathe who worship neither power nor its sublimation as History, the perhaps empty fidelity to self of a Julien or a Fabrizio will continue to draw readers, made, in

Valéry's phrase, *proud to be so.*

The sway of Stendhal's name reaches beyond individualism, or the Barresian *culte du moi,* it must be realized. The age of Gide may be over, and even that of Camus, whose lapidary style and devastatingly straightforward heroes hark back to Stendhal's in more than one way. Beckett, Sarraute, Ionesco have cut down the self to its nerve endings in tics, muffled flurries, garbled outbursts. Character is dissolved, language made autonomous, plot shuffled out of all temporality. The spirit of Stendhal, though not grossly perceptible in these laboratory putterings, hovers freely over the whole scene. The writer who mouthed none of the pieties of his trade, who neither sought to shock[4] nor feared to outrage, is not easily dismissed from the consciousness of an age concerned with disregarding all taboos, dispensing with all trodden paths, stripping away all the masks. An age that might do well to take to heart the admonition that behind every mask ... lies another mask, which Nietzsche may have learned from the example of Stendhal.[5]

The perennial youthfulness of the works of Stendhal may after all be an illusion: one hundred and thirty years is a short span indeed by which to measure a reputation, though perhaps no more should be required of a critic who cannot pose as seer than to attempt to sort out the strands of a writer's endurance to the day of present writing, noting its fluctuations, and making the soberest assessment of the utterly elusive future. Stendhal's major detractors are few (Henry James thought him utterly immoral), his admirers certainly worldwide. He has not been spared the embarrassment of open worship, in fact, and an impressive number of scholarly lives have been selflessly devoted to the decoding of his vile handwriting, the tracking down of his love affairs, the lovingly learned edition of all his scattered works (79 volumes in the Divan collection). Valéry chuckled at the thought of the learned tomes (which continue to pour out) devoted to every quirk of a mind that would have found so much gravity ludicrous. Yet we owe to scholars and exegetes a panoramic display of a lifework often willfully secreted, in that characteristic dialectic of *pudeur* and ostentation which sums up the writer's divided condition. From Taine's ascription to the man of an intuitive grasp of scientific principle in the creation of his characters to Gilbert Durand's analysis of the mythic features in *The Charterhouse of Parma,* literary scholarship has subjected his works to all the myriad variations of fashion and point of view spawned by a century of intensified attention to the recent past. The flow isn't about to cease, for the material is both elastic and durable. Beneath the swift course of the writings' smooth surface Georges Blin burrows into the maze of many-layered motivations, in psychoanalytic fashion, while at the other side of the intellectual spectrum Robert Vigneron diligently reconciles the conflicting models from Beyle's amorous experience, out of which the author Stendhal fashioned the heroines of his novels. And to endow the Babel Tower of learning and critical observation with the hair-raising splendor of the surreal, Fabrizio's ordeal after Waterloo has been obliquely compared, in one of the most impressive works devoted to Stendhal as a writer, to the fate of the legionnaires who served with Hitler's armies, under the regime of the Liberation!

There may be little point, after this recital of protean variation, to attempt to stake out a specifically Stendhalian territory on the slopes of Parnassus, to number in some ways the flocks of his ascertainable posterity. The once venerable belief in the reality of literary influences has by now all but joined belief in the astrology whence the term first derived. It was Gide who spoke the liberating word, when he posited that a writer above all *chooses* his own influences: that the waters flow back, so to speak, to their sources. It cannot be said that literary scholarship reeled all at once with the impact of this indictment of its cherished mechanistic assumptions, but within a few decades the lesson sank in, and ossification reversed its course: henceforward a writer is no longer computed as the sum of his sources, but as the nexus of his prophetic stirrings. Call Pascal an existentialist, read in him phenomenological anticipations, and you have saved his reputation for yet another decade! Though Stendhal has not escaped this imperative of updating (who would be so bold as to write a dissertation today in the vocabulary of yesterday's inquiries?), it is reassuring to note that curiosity regarding his political thinking (H.-F. Imbert, *Les Métamorphoses de la Liberté ou Stendhal devant la Restauration et le Risorgimento,* Paris: J. Corti, 1967) or his social preoccupations (F. Rude, *Stendhal et la pensée sociale de son temps,* Paris: Plon, 1967) has not been fully displaced by concern with myth and the philosophy of language (cf. Cl. Perruchot's brilliant exercise "Stendhal et le problème du langage," *French Review* [May 1968], 794 ff.).

Stendhal's reflections in the literature of our time, his *présence*, to use the serviceable French term, must not be looked for so much in conscious imitation (although Giono's *Hussard sur le toit* is an amazing tribute of this kind) or in traceable manner,[6] as in that much more fugitive aura Valéry so rightly described as his *tone.* I suppose the highest tribute that can be paid to a great master is to say that he has left the state of the art itself never to be as it had been before he put his mark upon it. Writing itself since *The Red and the Black* and *The Charterhouse of Parma* stands in an altered case. Never again may a writer dispense altogether with that distance, at once mocking and affectionate, which makes a character come to life as someone not wholly foreign to the author (Madame Bovary, c'est moi) though somehow held at arm's length. Or rather, since it certainly cannot be said that writers generally adopted this playful affectionate stance, the possibility looms on the horizon—and it will tinge the most unlikely performances (doesn't Leopold Bloom himself stride through his mediocre existence with something of the Stendhalian indomitable stride?).

Two examples chosen almost at random may help illustrate the diffuseness as well as the pervasiveness of the presence I have in mind. It may not occur at first blush to label E. M. Forster a Stendhalian. His concerns are far from heroic, the characters he deals with are fine but mostly wounded and retiring, his sense of mystery and of the dark forces quite remote from the Ideologues' calm reasonings. Still the tone is there, of a bantering seriousness, the much-shorn faith subsists in the prevalence of civilized will over dark unreason, the same troubled two cheers are uttered for democracy. But more telling than kinship are what I would call the workings of a Stendhalian dispensation. That irruption of the god Pan in the workaday fabric of existence, the echo of the Malabar caves or the raucously alive young athlete mowed down in his strength with telling unexpectedness, show to me the mark of Stendhal's commanding *disinvoltura*. The writer as demiurge has license to strike down, to kill off, to throw into panic his own creation with the smiling composure of a Jove, far removed from the lumbering gait and sweating countenance of the Balzacian-Dreiserian school, more closely akin to Vulcan. François Leuwen is killed off between chapters, Fabrizio escapes at a leap from the tower without the half-volume of buildup it might have cost the author, just as Mrs. Moore, though fated to become a goddess, steps grumpily into the steamer cabin from which she will issue no more.

At the zenith of the contemporary horizon shines the bright star of Vladimir Nabokov. He rightly claims kinship with the French novelists rather than the German expressionists, and makes no secret of his disaffection with the shade of Balzac. Rimbaud (rainbow) and Flaubert (Miss Emperor) reap the honors of his playful-sardonic acknowledgments far more conspicuously than Stendhal as far as I can tell (the terrain is mined, the reader advances at his peril). I have no hesitation at all, however, to assign to the dominion of Stendhal the cheerful (though bloodier) execution of heartless knaves and vixens (such as the German Mme Grandet in *King, Queen, Knave),* the jubilant exercise of an author's autocratic power, the deep *pudeur* of sentiment almost never spoken, artfully concealed in lepidopteral flight and lore, finally the imperial sway of taboo-crashing lovers, in *Ada,* trampling underfoot all limitations in the triumphant assertion of heart over matter.

Need one say more? But perhaps we owe Stendhal one last look at the configuration of traits to which may be attributed his tenacious hold over so many to this day. The quarrel between the Enlightenment and Romanticism could be outrageously simplified as the conflict between the head and the heart. Science, technology, the idea of progress reflect a faith that God's plan for mankind is to be read by the light of reason. Newton's plainly enunciated three laws of motion taught the age of Voltaire that while man could dispute forever about the mystery of Creation, the farthest recesses of the cosmos could be encompassed in a simple mathematical formula founded on exact observation and supported by verifiable data. The humble collaboration of the mind and the senses stood fair to deliver the secrets of nature over to man—both outward and inner nature, cleansed of the thick mold of ignorance and superstition designed to keep him in chains. Kings and priests were on the run: common sense in its homespun fustian, having taken the dazzle out of their pomp and their mysteries, prepared to set mankind free—to worship the God who had made the world in the image of reason, and all mankind both equal and prepared to be just, now that it was to be free.

All the truths which this elevating picture leaves out of the reckoning, the dark truths of the heart, the waywardness of the blood, the call of the Unknown and the recognition of transcendence, Romanticism made its own. Tension, dialectic, the divided self, the claims of energy and of passion (Blake's Proverbs of Hell) manifest themselves in the unfurling of a worldview which complements without effectively displacing the contrary views embodied in the progress of science—both natural and social science. The singularity of Stendhal, on the literary scene, comes as we have already shown, from that gift of fortune that reconciled in his breast the two sides of a divided inheritance. The wound sustained as a child from the untimely loss of a passionately beloved mother ranged him alone, rebellious, forever unreconciled to the dreary realm of the real, on the side of the dark angels, a Romantic to the core, for whom love, passion, energy could alone bring redemption. Italy reached on horseback, to the strains of Cimarosa, was to create the blend of heroism, music, and unsophisticated passion that represents his own variant on the Romantic dream. The quirk of fate which willed that his mother's surviving parent, Dr. Henri Gagnon, should have worn his considerable learning with a charm that blended the eighteenth-century spirit of the Enlightenment with the beloved maternal inheritance, made the world of science a matter of the heart. Hence the curiously emotional tinge attaching to mathematics, hence the happy day that took young Beyle to Paris on the wings of mathematical proficiency, hence the lifelong faith in the geometry of the senses wherewith this admirer of Helvetius and Destutt de Tracy sought to capture the dark secrets of the heart. Hence, most miraculous of all, those would-be calculators who are truly dreamers: Julien Sorel, Lucien Leuwen, Lamiel, Archbishop del Dongo . . .

Realism and Romanticism, the cool faith in what can be controlled and the feverish surrender to what lies beyond the will, are two modes of perceiving and delineating the world, while seeking to make one's peace with it, which have far from lost their sway on the contemporary scene. Science keeps forcing upon us greater rigor in our consideration even of questions of taste and style (the poets themselves these days sometimes write to suit the imagination of technicians), while the young grow hirsute, bow to gurus, and seek ecstasy in stupefaction. A writer who would seem to have a foot in both camps might appear to hold an unbreakable claim on universal popularity.

Stendhal's hold on his readers, I believe, proceeds from a less eclectic stance. The secret which his very personal fusion of Romanticism and the Enlightenment threatens to give away, and which gives an almost fortuitous psychic conjunction its extraordinary appeal, is that these two great moments in the consciousness of the West are not, as would on the surface appear, so much two steps locked in dialectical opposition as the two stages in a natural process of procreation. Romanticism is in every sense of the word the child of the Enlightenment. A certain youthful petulance, the adolescent's difficult relation to parent, a tendency to overreact to what nevertheless binds them together, even that precociously dejected pose that makes the father seem the youth by the side of his moody son, have long obscured the true state of the relationship. Yet if we consider how eighteenth-century *sentiment* flowers into romantic exuberance, how the cult of liberty gives rise to the demand for expressive freedom (Hugo's *J'ai mis un bonnet rouge au dictionnaire . . . "),* how the belief in progress spilled over into the affirmation that the men of today be free to think and feel the thoughts of today (Stendhal's definition of Romanticism in *Racine et Shakespeare)* we begin to see the deeper kinship of the two ages represented by Goethe in the birth of Euphorion from the union of Faust and Helen of Troy.

The novels of Stendhal, tales of the sublime knit together by the clear-eyed observation of things as they are, may well owe their powerful appeal to the inner cohesion they reveal between the head and the heart of our post-Enlightenment, post-Romantic culture, which still feeds more than it knows upon the rich remains of that half-buried giant carcass. Yet I prefer to leave the last word to the poet whom I have already quoted, to Paul Valéry, who said of Stendhal: *Il rend son lecteur fier de l'être.* For in the last analysis that tone of voice which is both tender and incisive, passionate and detached, indignant and amused is what makes of the reader of Stendhal the spell-bound companion of a man who wrote *pour se désennuyer*, to keep himself amused, and to whom he owes—along with the headiest companionship—that inestimable boon for himself.

Notes and References

Prologue

1. Mathilde Dembowski had died in 1825, in her thirty-fifth year.
2. *OI* (Pléiade) 26-32.
3. *Op. cit.*, p. 26.
4. *Ibid.*
5. *OI,* 14.
6. *OI,* 32. (*God* is in English in the French text, misspelled English being an important feature of his code language.)
7. *OI,* 1525-1530.
8. *OI,* 1434.

Chapter One

1. A procedure initiated in I. Howe's suggestive article, "Stendhal: the Politics of Survival," reprinted in *Stendhal, A Collection of Critical Essays,* edited by V. Brombert (Prentice Hall, 1962).
2. The Revolution of 1830 obligingly disposed of the Restoration monarchy in the interval of writing and publication: a rare conjunction of art and reality.
3. Stendhal's complex ambivalence toward his heroes—masterfully laid out by V. Brombert in *La Voie Oblique* (Paris: P.U.F., 1954)—is clearly demonstrated by his own unflattering assessment of the victory bulletins in *Henry Brulard:* "Posterity will never know what vile ninnies the heroes of those bulletins of Napoleon were, and how I laughed as I received the *Moniteur* in Vienna, Dresden, Berlin, Moscow, which reached almost no one in the army, lest they scoff at its lies." (*OI,* 195)
4. The first condition he set on "taking service," the fruit no doubt of his reading of the *Confessions* (the work of a man who had indeed worn a livery)! Raw pride was to be a curiously effective asset in an environment too gross to detect intangibles. When Julien, outraged by his master's boorish tone, makes a scene with the object of obtaining an apology, M. de Rênal can only imagine that he has a better offer elsewhere (how

otherwise could a young peasant talk back to his employer?) and sighingly fetches him another raise in salary.

5. Stendhal here endowed Julien with greater courage than he has had himself when he, under less extreme circumstances, lamentably fumbled what he took to be his chance to seduce Countess Daru, during his stay at her chateau. ("The army I commanded was full of terror and thought the undertaking beyond its strength of character. This is what I said to myself with rage on May 3rd while walking alone in the park at quarter past eleven, after everyone had gone to bed.") *OI (Journal),* 1024.

6. His brothers, like Joseph's, left him for dead after meeting him in his genteel tutor's garb.

7. Gilbert Durand has given a brilliant account of fixed stages in the epic career of the Stendhalian myth hero in *Le Décor mythique de la Chartreuse de Parme* (Paris, 1961).

8. Pascal had left his mark on a movement that Stendhal quaintly revives in his rather literary treatment of clerical infighting in the nineteenth century. The Jansenists had fought a losing battle for principle against expediency. Their morals were pure, their views disinterested if misguided, their cause, associated with uncompromising opposition, ruthlessly smothered: no more was needed to turn the persecuted *abbés* Chélan and Pirard, the clerical mentors of Julien and the upholders of a *clean* religion, into the anachronistic martyrs of a seventeenth-century faith.

9. Pale and slight, Julien kept repeating: "Sir, I despise you," as the huge coachman bellowed his obscenities.

10. Named after "the incomparable Gros ..., geometer of the first class and my master, unbeknownst to my male relatives, for he was a Jacobin and my whole family fanatically *ultra.*" *OI, Brulard,* 18.

11. A technical term invented by Stendhal, in the little treatise *On Love,* to designate with scientific precision the maturation, in the unconscious, of the full-blown love arising from shattered seeds of casual encounter.

12. That monarch shared with Lyndon Johnson a reputation for astute political manipulation and the savage enmity of artists and writers. (Béranger made his inflated reputation by lampooning him; Daumier immortalized his pear-shaped features.)

13. Sartre's Hugo, in *Red Gloves,* springs to mind: he counters the antagonism of his proletarian fellow Party members, children of hunger, with the tale of his own childhood, matching their deprivation with his loveless force-feeding.

14. That prototype of modern guerilla or brush wars, Napoleon's unsuccessful bid to force the nineteenth century upon the Spanish populace, is a superb emblem of Mosca's tortuous political position: he earned his perilous Liberal credentials in a war that opposed him to the people's (unenlightened) will.

15. The nineteenth-century French equivalent of the far right, the

party that looked *ultra montes* (beyond the Alps) to Papal supremacy: hence an epithet of disparagement to tick off all reactionaries.

Chapter Two

1. "Who does not know," writes Montaigne (in D. Frame's translation), that in the school of Love "they proceed contrary to all order? Study, exercise, practice are ways leading to incapacity; the novices there give the lessons." *Essays,* III:5, 684 (Stanford, 1958).

2. Whose uncompromising doctrine of papal supremacy, *Du Pape,* scaled heights of self-parody that made it a fit screen for Julien's earnest joke on his times.

3. An image borrowed by Stendhal in his little treatise *On Love* from the custom of miners at Hallstein, near Salzburg, of dropping a leafless bough into the salt mine. After a couple of months, the bough would be recovered, glittering with the diamonds of crystal formation.

4. Had he had breath enough and sense, at nineteen, he might have taken for himself Stendhal's own reflection on the day his struggle for the long-delayed possession of Angelina Pietragrua had ended in victory: "My happiness is complete, except for the one thing that would make it happiness for a fool: that it is a victory." *(OI, Journal,* 1118.)

5. A daughter was clearly unthinkable.

6. It should be noted that the Green Huntsman café also makes an appearance on the outskirts of Koenigsberg in the unfinished novella on a German theme: *The Rose and the Green.*

7. It is noteworthy that Lucien had to be fortified, in his coldness to the now groveling beauty, by the memory of her cruel jibes against the naked wretches victimized by the regime, as she turned down a charitable solicitation on their behalf.

8. Du Poirier's close relative!

Chapter Three

1. Julien, as an artist, can master only the *language* of these foes of all decency and straightforwardness: the maundering, long-winded, evasive tirades by which they keep each other at bay in a ballet of noncommittal repartee. Witness the childish glee with which he greets his success (Penguin, 153) at out-Jesuiting Valenod's emissary, neither accepting nor refusing to take up a post with the poorhouse director's children.

2. Julien faints with terror: he is the only man, with his own father, who ever strikes fear into that bold heart.

3. Charles X, the reigning Bourbon king, had been deposed by the July Revolution, in favor of the Orléans branch, descended from Louis XIV's

younger brother and represented by Louis-Philippe.

4. A distinction forcefully developed by Bernanos, in *The Diary of a Country Priest* (New York: Macmillan, 1937), pp. 244-45.

5. The *conceit* of the enormously vain cripple is taken up again by Stendhal in the figure of the hunchback Dr. Sansfin, in *Lamiel*, who lays claim quite unsmilingly to the reputation of a Don Juan.

6. One of the charming touches in which all these traits are allowed to blend in with his genuine affection for his noble-born young vicar is the nineteen-page Latin letter he sends Fabrizio in his hiding place, following the slaying of Giletti, setting out the full political implications of that affair (i.e. the barefaced frameup of Fabrizio by the Prince of Parma). In it "the words corresponding to 'our Sovereign Lord' and 'feigns that belief' were in Greek, and Fabrizio felt infinitely obliged to the Archbishop for having had the courage to write them" (221).

Chapter Four

1. Modeled after Stendhal's own English teacher, the Irish monk Father Iéky.

2. Mathematics, like the Army, was a poetic rather than a practical outlook for Stendhal: hence the saving ambivalence which sent him to Paris bound for the Polytechnique where nonetheless he failed to apply, and which made of his days in the cavalry a sequence of leaves eventuating in sudden resignation (like Lucien's after Nancy).

3. As Stendhal himself had noted, in *Memoirs of a Tourist;* but then, he reflected, if Balzac wrote more simply, would the provincials read him?

4. "Oftentimes, to describe happiness is for me to dilute it," *OI, Journal,* 1166.

5. *Supra,* Ch. 1, note 5.

6. The Swedish film *Dear John,* though both mawkish and stolid, has the merit of facing the issue squarely: there is more to bringing man and woman together in bed than either cynics or romantics can tell us.

7. " 'I pay great attention to the fortunes of my house, I can advance them considerably; I take care of my pleasures too, and that's a thing of the first importance—at least in my eyes,' he added, surprising a look of astonishment in Father Pirard's. Although a man with plenty of common sense, the abbé was amazed to find an old man talking so openly of his pleasures" (Penguin, 224).

8. He tells the story at lunch time of his fall from horseback in the morning. " 'I have good hopes of this young priest,' the Marquis said to the academician. 'A provincial showing simplicity on such an occasion! that's a thing that has never been seen before, and never will be again. And on top of it all he relates his misadventure in front of the *ladies!*' " (262).

9. Louise Varèse translates *créancier* as *debtor,* thus blunting Leuwen's little joke. *(Green Huntsman, 5)*

Chapter Five

1. Henri Martineau gives a vigorous refutation of these views in his indispensable *L'Œuvre de Stendhal* (Paris: Albin Michel, 1951), pp. 400–410.

2. The death of Leuwen *père* also hits the reader totally unprepared, at the height of the man's powers, at the point when he eclipses the hero himself.

3. Fabrizio too will learn to read from the storied *Genealogy* of the Del Dongo family.

4. In the narrator's reflections on Stendhal and Dostoevski, spoken to Albertine, which are among the forerunners of the present-day thematic vogue *(La Prisonnière* (Pléiade edition), III, 377).

5. See his little joke, Ch. II, p. 31 *supra*.

6. The massacre of the Rue Transnonain, immortalized by Daumier's drawing, is still fresh in Lucien's memory, with its unarmed workers, women, and children slaughtered indiscriminately by the troops under orders.

Epilogue

1. "God's only excuse is that He doesn't exist," is Stendhal's most celebrated *mot* on the subject.

2. "What a mass of bold sayings I put forward tremblingly!" *(OI, Egotisme,* 1460).

3. Having spent some of his last months reworking the novel to the master's misleading specifications, happily to no conclusion.

4. Georges Blin has documented the quite unexpected restraint of that outspoken iconoclast, from first draft to finished love scene.

5. Taught perhaps himself by Pascal's "if habit be a second nature, is then perhaps nature a first habit?"

6. Isn't it remarkable that the master of the *pastiche*, Marcel Proust, who spared neither his beloved Saint-Simon nor his much-admired Balzac, left Stendhal unparodied?

Selected Bibliography

(Unless otherwise specified place of publication is Paris for French works, New York for works in English.)

PRIMARY SOURCES

I. EDITIONS IN FRENCH (SETS)

Correspondance. 3 vols. Gallimard, 1962-68. (Bibliothèque de la Pléiade.)
Œuvres, ed. V. del Litto and E. Abravanel. Lausanne: Editions Rencontre, 1960-.
Œuvres complètes, ed. E. Champion and P. Arbelet. 34 vols. Librairie Champion, 1913-1940.
Œuvres intimes. Gallimard, 1955. (Bibliothèque de la Pléiade.)
Romans et nouvelles. 2 vols. Gallimard, 1952. (Bibliothèque de la Pléiade.)
In addition, there is the fabulous 79-volume edition brought out between 1927 and 1937 by Henri Martineau at Le Divan, complete, though it came out title by title, without a general *Œuvres complètes* heading.

II. EDITIONS IN FRENCH OF THE MAJOR NOVELS

La Chartreuse de Parme, ed. H. Martineau. Garnier, 1961. (Classiques Garnier.)
Lucien Leuwen. Le Livre de Poche, 1960.
Le Rouge et le Noir, ed. H. Martineau. Garnier, 1960. (Classiques Garnier.)

III. ENGLISH TRANSLATIONS

A. Major movels:
The Charterhouse of Parma, trans. C. K. Scott Moncrieff. Doubleday, 1956. (Anchor book.)
The Green Huntsman, trans. L. Varèse. New Directions, 1950. *(Lucien*

Leuwen, Part I.)

Scarlet and Black, trans. M. R. B. Shaw. Baltimore, 1953. I much prefer it
    to the next item. *The Red and the Black,* Trans., C. K. Scott Moncrieff.
    Modern Library, 1926.

The Telegraph, trans., L. Varèse. New Directions, 19 50. *(Lucien Leuwen,*
    Part II.)

B. Other works:

Armance. Chester Springs: Dufour, 1961.

Feder, trans. H. R. Edwards. Chester Springs: Dufour, 1962.

Lamiel, trans., T. W. Earp. New Directions, 1952.

The Life of Henry Brulard. Pleasantville: Funk & Wagnalls, 1968.

Memoirs of a Tourist. Evanston: Northwestern University Press, 1962.

On Love. Black & Gold Library, n.d.

Private Diaries. Norton, 1962.

Roman Journal, ed. H. Chevalier. Collier, 1961.

Shorter Novels, trans. C. K. Scott Moncrieff. Black & Gold Library, n.d.

SECONDARY SOURCES

I. WORKS IN ENGLISH

ADAMS, R. M. *Stendhal.* London: Merlin Press, 1959. Short and readable,
    almost rambunctious in liveliness, it takes the reader painlessly through
    a vast tract of Stendhalian learning.

ATHERTON, JOHN. *Stendhal.* London: Bowes & Bowes, 1965. Gives a
    lively and compendious account of man and works, organized along
    lines not unlike my own.

BROMBERT, VICTOR. *Stendhal.* Prentice-Hall, 1962. An anthology of
    critical writings which includes in English translation such capital essays
    as Auerbach's piece from *Mimesis,* a chapter from Jean Prévost's great
    book, pages by Starobinski and Jean-Pierre Richard among others.

GREEN, F. C. *Stendhal.* Cambridge University Press, 1939. Presents the
    life and the works in some detail, sensibly and authoritatively set out.

HEMMINGS, F. W. J. *Stendhal—A Study of His Novels.* Oxford:
    Clarendon Press, 1964. Proceeds more sedately than Adams, but no less
    instructively and sure-footedly.

JOSEPHSON, MATTHEW. *Stendhal.* Doubleday, 1946. Provides a leisure-
    ly and thoughtful biography, complete with a delineation of the plots
    of the novels interestingly and comprehensively commented upon.

II. FRENCH CRITICISM AND SCHOLARSHIP

Among the works in French the selection must be ruthless. The works
cited are merely the top layer, resting on mountains of uncited first-rate
scholarship, to give the reader an inkling of scope only.

ALAIN (EMILE CHARTIER.) *Stendhal.* Presses Universitaires de France, 1948. The reflections on Stendhal of the man who was the intellectual conscience of the Third Republic.

ALBERES, F. M. *Le Naturel chez Stendhal.* Nizet, 1956. An exhaustive study of a central feature of the Stendhalian canon.

BARDECHE, MAURICE. *Stendhal romancier.* Table Ronde, 1947. Indispensable. With Prévost's the best study of the art of the novelist.

BLIN, GEORGES. *Stendhal et les problèmes du roman.* J. Corti, 1954. *Stendhal et les problèmes de la personnalité.* J. Corti, 1958. Together these two works constitute an exhaustive search for the deeper links of psyche and creation.

BLUM, LÉON. *Stendhal et le beylisme.* Albin Michel, 1947. First published in 1914 by a man who was to be France's first Socialist Premier, it is a pioneering work on the Stendhalian outlook.

BOURGET, PAUL. "Stendhal," *Essais de Psychologie contemporaine.* A. Lemerre, 1890. The celebrated portrait that rekindled Stendhal's fame.

BROMBERT, VICTOR. *Stendhal et la voie oblique.* New Haven: Yale University Press, 1954. A masterful study which ferrets out the writer's strategy of hit-and-run defense of his beloved heroes against the reader's anticipated derogation.

DEL LITTO, VICTOR. *La Vie intellectuelle de Stendhal.* Presses Universitaires de France, 1959. A monumental account of readings and sources.

IMBERT, H.–F. *Les Métamorphoses de la liberté ou Stendhal devant la Restauration et le Risorgimento.* J. Corti, 1967. Indispensable study of Stendhal's political evolution.

MARTINEAU, HENRI. *Le Cœur de Stendhal.* Albin Michel, 1952, 1953. The authoritative biography.

–––. *L'Œuvre de Stendhal.* Albin Michel, 1951. The genesis and avatars of each of the works.

–––. *Petit Dictionnaire stendhalien.* Le Divan, 1948. Lists names, nicknames, and pseudonyms referred to in his writings, giving all the biographical information available.

PREVOST, JEAN. *La Création chez Stendhal.* Mercure de France, 1951. If you read only one book on Stendhal, let it be this one.

RUDE, F. *Stendhal et la pensée sociale de son temps.* Plon, 1967. Does justice to an important aspect of Stendhal's preoccupations.

TAINE, HIPPOLYTE. "Stendhal," *Nouveaux Essais de critique et d'histoire.* Hachette, 1909. The trail-blazing 1864 essay.

VALERY, PAUL. "Stendhal," *Variété* II. Gallimard, 1930. Lucid and playful.

Index

(The works of Stendhal are listed under his name)

Index